# Haunted
# East Anglia

### Joan Forman

D1336144

Jarrold Colour Publications, Norwich

First published in Great Britain by Robert Hale and Company 1974
First published in Fontana 1976. Second Impression March 1977
First published by Jarrold and Sons Ltd 1985

Printed in Great Britain by Jarrold and Sons Ltd, Norwich. 185

ISBN 0–7117–0178–4

*For Thelma*                                    Opposite: *Hickling Broad*


## Author's Note

Since the first edition of *Haunted East Anglia* in 1974, several minor changes have occurred for which the author is not responsible but of which nevertheless she feels readers may wish to take note.

Over the eleven-year period since the book's first publication, time and chance have made a few alterations to some of the facts contained within it. These do not concern the hauntings themselves, for ghosts are oblivious to time and (almost) impervious to chance. However, living humans are not so lucky. Thus, several of the persons named as percipients in these accounts have now moved away from the area of their experiences and live elsewhere, their places having been taken by others who may or may not be living with phantoms. In particular, this effect is noticeable in the management of hotels and inns, where the incumbents move fairly regularly.

Other changes of personnel may have arisen as a result of a percipient's death or the simple fact of house-removal. People no longer follow the traditions of their fathers by spending a whole lifetime in one place.

Any reader, therefore, who decides to visit one of the haunted sites mentioned in the following pages is asked to remember that the person who originally told me the story may by now be over the hills and far away. However, except in a few rare cases, this fact is unlikely to have affected the ghosts, who are always more concerned with places than people. The hauntings will be where they always were. And no doubt new folk will be experiencing them in the old surroundings.

                                                        Joan Forman.
Norfolk. January 1985.


## Acknowledgements

*The research and writing of this book occupied me for over a year and during that time I talked to and interviewed nearly two hundred people. Almost without exception, my enquiries were received warmly and with courtesy, and I was granted every facility which might assist me in the task of discovering and (where possible) analysing the ghost stories of the East Anglian region.*

*To single out individuals for particular acknowledgement would be an invidious and hopeless task, for the response to my questions was invariably interested, good-humoured and helpful. The persons concerned in the various happenings seemed as anxious as I to discover the real nature of what had occurred or of what they knew.*

*I should like, therefore, to express my thanks to the many people who wrote, telephoned or talked to me, who gave unhesitatingly of their time, and who took pains to research for me details which were obscure. My gratitude must also include the kind persons who unhesitatingly gave me permission to enter their homes or property in connection with my investigations. I hope that all concerned will find in this book a few answers to the questions we have all asked.*

*I also wish to acknowledge the permission of Mrs George Bambridge, Macmillan of London & Basingstoke and Macmillan Co. of Canada to quote from Rudyard Kipling's 'A Smuggler's Song' on pages 50 and 51 and that of Messrs Faber and Faber to quote from T. S. Eliot's 'Burnt Norton' from Collected Poems 1909–1962 on page 108.*

# Contents

# Introduction

To haunt, according to the *Concise Oxford Dictionary*, is to visit or frequent, to stay habitually, and this term may equally be applied to the living, who habitually visit certain areas, and to so-called 'ghosts' or manifestations of the dead which appear persistently to frequent particular places.

Any writer who undertakes a book dealing with hauntings must, at some stage, declare himself to be either convinced or sceptical on the subject of ghosts. One plumps for the first or the second, depending on personal experience. Those who have had encounters with the inexplicable are likely to believe in psychic phenomena; those who have not, frequently take an 'I'll believe it when I see it' attitude.

Yet the incidence of psychic experience is higher than one would suppose. During the course of my investigations, I found some reluctance to reveal experiences, partly through fear of ridicule, as though the occurrences were so rare and the victim so set apart, that neither would be believed if the incidents were publicly narrated. I am not convinced that psychic manifestations are rare. In fact I would put the ratio of those who have, against those who have not encountered them, as high as one person in three. Ghosts and their habits seem to be a pretty common phenomenon.

In a few instances, people who had encountered psychic manifestation and were kind enough to narrate their experiences to me, requested that their names (or more rarely, addresses) be withheld. To this I agreed, respecting the reasons given for the desire for anonymity. I have therefore substituted pseudonyms where appropriate, and these are marked with an asterisk throughout the text. Most of those interviewed, however, had no objection to the use of proper names and places.

For the purposes of this book I have taken the region of East Anglia to include the counties of Norfolk, Lincolnshire, Suffolk, Essex, Hertfordshire, Huntingdonshire, Northamptonshire, with Cambridgeshire and the Isle of Ely taken as one unit. This is roughly the area covered by the BBC's broadcasting range across its East Anglian region. I have excluded Bedfordshire (which the BBC included) because it does not seem to me to fit naturally into the distinctive nature of the East Anglian region.

Wherever possible, I have chosen stories of experiences within the present century, though this does not mean that the *earliest recorded experience* of a particular haunting is that of the twentieth century. However, it seems to me that contemporary, and if possible first- or second-hand experience is likely to be more valid and more valuable than hoary accounts resuscitated from long-dead authors and long-forgotten books. So my human source material in the main is living contemporary and most of the experiences described are comparatively recent.

During the book's writing, I have had a number of curious encounters of my own. Having both Scottish and Irish blood in my ancestry, I have never been sceptical on the subject of hauntings. But had I been so, the year's work on East Anglian ghosts would have convinced me of my error.

# NORFOLK
## A Tolling Bell, a Chair and the Portrait of a Lady

Norfolk is a county rich in historical association (though ghostly mani-festations are not necessarily a legacy from the ancient past) and although it has its share of banal hauntings – the coaches and horses, clanking chains, and spectral black dogs which turn up all over Britain – there are also unusual and interesting ghosts, perpetuating an individuality which marks out a particular time, place or set of circumstances, distinguishing them as belonging to *this* county and no other.

Occasionally more than one manifestation occurs in a particular area, apparently without any connection between the incidents. For instance, at least two ghosts are recorded on Hickling Broad, one male, one female.

Several times in the course of the last hundred and fifty years, the figure of a man has been seen, dressed in soldier's uniform of the Napoleonic Wars, and skating rapidly across Hickling as though its surface were frozen.

As anyone who has visited them knows, the Norfolk Broads are man-made inland lakes, reed-fringed, wild bird-haunted, with thin belts of trees backing the reeds. They are fed and emptied by a network of lakes and streams and the whole area is reminiscent of the old lost fenland.

The origin of the skating soldier is known. Apparently during the wars with France in the early nineteenth century, a young soldier was stationed with his regiment in north Norfolk. He formed an attachment to a local girl whose home was on the far side of Hickling Broad, and the couple were only able to meet when the young man was not on duty. The winter was hard that year, and the Broads were frozen for much of the season. It was therefore easy for the boy to don skates and skim across the great mere in the dusk. Night after night when he was free to do so, he visited the house on the far shore of the Broads, his skates singing over the ice, his movements free and vigorous in the sharp air. The frost persisted and the ice remained deep and firm, until almost winter's end. Then the temperature rose a little.

Whether or not the soldier was warned of the danger, we cannot now tell; whether or not he tried the ice before setting out on his last journey across Hickling, there is no record. One imagines he must have been satisfied of its safety, at least near the banks, for he started out as usual, vigorously, no doubt enjoying the physical movement. He was halfway across when he hit a soft patch of ice. It cracked beneath him, and he fell through into the water and drowned.

From time to time over the last century and a half, the figure of the soldier has appeared, skating rhythmically and vigorously over Hickling Broad's surface, as he did until the moment the ice gave beneath him.

Hickling's other manifestation is less well known, but the following experience occurred to some friends of a near neighbour of mine. The people in question were spending a holiday aboard a cruiser on Hickling, and had meant to move the boat to a berth on the far side of the Broad before dark so that they might make an early start in the morning in the direction they intended to follow. However, a series of delays took place during the evening and darkness had fallen before they were ready to take the cruiser across the lake to its new mooring.

They were well aware of the waterway ruling that forbids the moving of craft by night. Such rules are necessary if danger to other boats is to be avoided. This particular couple were experienced and confident of their ability to handle the boat in the dark; they decided to ignore the regulation.

The cruiser drew away from the bank and headed out into open water. They were almost halfway over, when the man caught sight of a dim shape appearing out of the darkness. Peering ahead, he could just distinguish the form of a punt, and a figure in a white dress, standing in it, poling the craft along. She was approaching their bows when he saw her, and he yelled at her to get clear. The woman neither changed her course nor replied to his frantic shout. For a few seconds he was convinced his craft had run her down. Then the punt and its occupant appeared on the other side of his vessel. The woman poled off into the darkness ignoring the cruiser, and the continued shouts of warning. The boat's owner had had a severe shock and both he and his wife were unnerved by the narrow escape from a possibly serious accident.

As soon as they had the cruiser safely berthed, they felt the need of a good stiff drink, and leaving the boat, walked to the nearest pub. Once inside, they poured out the story of the reckless woman in the punt to the landlord. He served them both before he expressed an opinion, then said, non-committally, 'Shouldn't worry too much if I were you. You didn't see a live woman in a real punt, you saw the local ghost. She poles from a mill on one side the Broad to a mill on the other. She always wears a white dress. There's nothing to worry about.' Her victims found this cold comfort.

I have not been able to discover the history of the punting woman. No doubt in life her journeys to and fro by punt were regular enough to constitute a habit. This repetition of what was in life a regular practice is a feature of many ghost stories. It is as though a pattern or rhythm had been developed and superimposed upon the material surroundings, so that when the instigator of the pattern was no longer able to carry it out, some imprint of the sequence still remained in the physical surroundings. I hope to return later to this aspect of hauntings and to consider the possible meaning of it.

The theory of a regular physical practice developing a surviving psychic pattern does not always hold, however. Occasionally a haunting represents a straight narration of events which took place in actual time, once and only once. Such is the story told me by a retired police constable who, at the time of his particular experience, was stationed at Northwold.

PC 91 Williams* had patrolled country beats for over twelve years, and had never during that time encountered anything which could not be explained by factual or physical means. Williams was a practical man, not given to imaginative flights, and believing in what he actually saw rather than in what he was told or what he heard by way of gossip. He was married, living in the local police house about three miles from Didlington Hall, and he was constable to four parishes, the most rural of which was Didlington. It was a hamlet only, a collection of scattered farm cottages, one farm and the village church. Its total population numbered just over eighty persons.

Some ten years previously the owner of Didlington Hall had died and the cemetery in which he buried lies only a short distance from the Hall.

It was a cold night and Constable Williams found his heavy serge overcoat inadequate to keep out the cutting wind. He glanced at his watch, shining the powerful hand torch on to the dial. The time was 22.50 hours. He calculated that if he cycled slowly he should reach Didlington Church at 23.00 hours, which would complete his last round at Didlington before moving on to another parish for his final tour of duty for that night. It was not a good night to be out in the open. Didlington is a heavily wooded area and the wind whistled between the avenues of trees on either side of the lane.

Williams was about to mount his bicycle when he heard a sound which made him pause. At first he thought it was the noise of the wind through the woodland; then as the sound was repeated he recognized it as that of a clanging bell. It occurred to him that it must be the chiming of the church clock, until he remembered that the church clock had not worked for years; it was stuck permanently at seven o'clock.

He jumped on his bicycle and pedalled in the direction of the church. The bell continued to ring sonorously as he rode, and he counted twenty-five tolls. It was certainly the bell of Didlington Church. As he reached the church gate, the ringing abruptly ceased, and the silence which followed it was more alarming than the previous din. There was no sound now apart from the wind in the trees and the snapping of small pieces of decayed wood as the constable moved into the church pathway.

Various possibilities occurred to him as he walked up the path under the overhanging elms. It could be a village joker playing games with him; or children larking with the bell. But not at this hour, and not on a night like this. However, something or someone had caused the half-ton bell to swing and it was his job to investigate the occurrence.

The church door was locked, but he knew the key was usually left under the doormat, and with the aid of his torch he located and fitted it into the lock. He turned the key with care, trying to make as little noise as possible in order not to alert any intruder who might be within.

Having unlocked the door, he swung it open as far as it would go, at the same time flashing on his torch and shining it over the pews, down the nave and under the belfry, where he knew the bell-rope hung. He saw the bell-rope and then felt the hair prickle on his scalp. *The rope was still swinging*; it was as though it had only a moment before been released by whoever was holding it. Yet there was not a soul in sight.

*Didlington Church*

The constable's mouth went dry. He had a feeling of being not alone. He was glad to grasp the handlebars of his bicycle, as a familiar, reassuring physical fact, and he pedalled back to the police house without completing the last leg of his beat. His wife noticed his shocked state and remarked that he looked as though he had seen a ghost. 'Perhaps I have,' he replied and then proceeded to tell her of his experience.

Some days later PC Williams met an aged parishioner who once worked at Didlington Hall. Without mentioning the earlier happenings he asked the old man the date on which the previous owner of Didlington had died.

'It was on the fourteenth day of November,' came the reply.

The entry in the policeman's notebook for the fateful night read laconically 'Patrolled Didlington. Examined Church.' The entry was dated 14 November 1956.

I have related the story as it was told to me by the police constable in question. Williams is not his real name, but he assures me that the facts are exactly as given here. As far as I can ascertain, he is the only person to have had this particular experience. Presumably he was in the right place at the right time to receive the manifestation.

I have not been able to conjecture why some areas contain a plurality of hauntings while others have no record at all of such occurrences. It is true, however, that if a place reports one ghost, you are likely to hear of others in the same district; yet villages on either side may have nothing of the kind.

The charming village of Brooke, south of Norwich, and one of the county's show villages, holds two or three good stories.

Mr Upton, a lively old gentleman of 85, with a rich Norfolk voice and a mind not at all clouded by years, gave me an account of experiences within his own family.

In his youth, Mr Upton was an ostler, an almost forgotten trade now, but one which until the beginning of the last war was still commonly practised in farming. Mr Upton looked after the farm's horses, and it was part of his duties to go the rounds of the stables at night before he left the farm.

On the night in question, he had gone into the horse-yard to check the animals before leaving, when he heard a rattling sound approaching down the hill outside the farmyard gate. It was a minute or two before he could identify the noise, but he decided it must be an old bicycle of the kind used before the invention of pneumatic tyres. In fact it was apparent from the sound that the machine had the hard steel rims of the earliest bicycles.

Mr Upton's first reaction was surprise that anyone near Brooke High Green should possess such a cycle. His second was curiosity about its owner. He turned away from the stables and watched the lane, waiting for the bicycle to pass so that he could identify the rider. The rattling came down the hill, growing louder as it drew nearer; it passed the farm gate, and to Mr Upton's discomfort, turned and retraced its route. Discomfort? The fact was that nothing visible had passed the farm gate. The bicycle could be heard but not seen. The old ostler swears that although it was dark, he would certainly have seen anything pass the gate, so near was he to it at the time. 'That was the sound of an old bone-shaker,' he said.

Two of his sisters encountered what appears to have been the same machine while they themselves were out cycling. They were approaching Swainsthorpe, when one of the women saw an old bicycle turning into a wood crowning a hilltop just ahead of them. 'Look at that old bicycle going there!' she cried excitedly to her sister. But the sister saw nothing at all, neither did she hear anything. The remarkable thing about this sighting was that the bicycle appeared to be riderless.

An even stranger experience occurred to another inhabitant of the same village. Mr Walker, a middle-aged man with a busy working life and a strictly practical approach to it, had occasion two years ago to meet a business acquaintance in Bungay on the Norfolk-Suffolk borders. He arranged to meet his friend in a local pub, and after the business had been transacted Mr Walker set out for home. The time was about 10.15 p.m. The night was dark but luminous, so that it was not strictly necessary to use full headlights on the car. However, there was little traffic on the road and Mr Walker had the car's lights full on so that the road ahead was clearly illuminated. The journey was perfectly unremarkable until he reached the stretch of new concrete road between Ditchingham and Bungay. At this point, the old road, bypassed by the new, veers away at the bottom of a hill to become a lay-by. Mr Walker crested the hill at about 40 m.p.h. and began the descent; the road ahead of him was empty and bright in the headlamps. The next moment he saw a coach and horses careering towards him on the crest of the road. His mind noted that there were four horses, that the coachman had some person seated beside him, and that a carriage lamp hung either side the vehicle. This much he saw before his brain registered that he and the coach were on a collision course. He braked sharply, but the other vehicle came on. Then he accelerated in an attempt to pass the coach; and at that point it swung away – 'floated away', to use Mr Walker's words – in front of him into the lay-by. He travelled home in a state of great agitation, the hair rising on his scalp. So unnerved was he by the experience that this ordinarily practical and unimaginative man had to be given a drink of brandy when he arrived home.

Some time later Mr Walker mentioned the stretch of road in question to an elderly local resident who knew the area well. The man's answer was to tell him that the place was called 'Lion's Grave' and was regarded as an evil place. 'Grave' in Norfolk means literally a hole in the ground. To the identity of 'Lion' or 'the lion' there is as yet no clue.

I should like to stress again that the man who underwent this experience is a balanced, matter-of-fact, perfectly logical individual. He finds the lack of physical explanation for his experience distasteful and embarrassing. He had to be pressed to give me the above information and would clearly have preferred to forget the whole strange incident.

The village of Brooke boasts several old houses, among them one which was formerly owned by the agent for a local estate. The house had originally been two cottages, but had been knocked into one to allow more space for the owner and his two adult daughters, both of whom were teachers. In time the family died out, the two old schoolteachers being the last to go. The house was sold and the new owners moved in. They stayed only a few months before leaving for newer property a short distance away.

It seems that the new people discovered they were not the only occupants of the house. On one occasion, the wife went into the bedroom and saw a female figure lying on the bed. She thought it was a trick of the light and dismissed the matter as an illusion. However, when the incident was repeated, she became unnerved, and the couple decided to leave the property.

The house stood empty for some time and then was bought by a Mr and Mrs Macdonald.* For a while nothing untoward occurred, then Mrs Macdonald had a strange experience with her alarm clock. She wound it up as usual and placed it on the bedside table. However, some hours later, the clock was found

*Brooke Village*

on the bedroom floor in a different part of the room. Neither husband nor wife had touched it, and no one else had been in the house.

On another occasion Mrs Macdonald had intended to call on an elderly neighbour. On entering her sitting-room before going out, she was surprised to see what she took to be that same neighbour seated in a chair in the room. She spoke to the woman, saying that she had been intending to visit her, when to her astonishment she saw the chair was empty. She recalled afterwards that the woman was wearing a long green dress and was 'a little old lady with white hair'. On reflection, the Macdonalds concluded that their visitor bore a strong resemblance to one of the two old ladies who used to teach school in the house.

My informant, who knew the house and had several times visited it, stated that whenever she was in the sitting-room she experienced a cold draught in the spot where the seated figure had been seen.

When the Macdonalds left, the house again stood empty. It was eventually bought by a family where there were children, and since that time the ghost has not reappeared. The two old ladies were, you will remember, schoolteachers and loved children. Both the families who experienced visitations were childless couples. Presumably the ghost is now satisfied to have children about the house again.

A strange story was related by an acquaintance of mine, a Mrs June Bennett.* At the time of the incidents with which her story is concerned, Mrs Bennett had been married only a short time. Both she and her husband had previously been married, and this was a second union for both of them. June had left the south of England to move into her husband's home at Wroxham in Norfolk – a home which had also been that of Mr Bennett's first wife.

The latter had been particularly devoted to and possessive of her home. She had, in fact, died in the house. The new wife paid no attention to this, however, as the circumstances are common, and there was nothing she could do at that time to change them. She felt in any case perfectly able to deal with any disturbing associations which might arise.

The couple had been married exactly a month when they arrived at Wroxham, and almost immediately the bride began to notice inexplicable occurrences in the house. Footsteps sounded on the stairs as though someone were walking up and down them; most disconcerting of all, peculiar smells arose in various rooms. When asked to describe the smells, Mrs Bennett was unable to do so. She could say only that they were like incense, and yet unlike. She had encountered nothing in her lifetime which exactly corresponded to these smells.

Although June Bennett spent much time along in the house, she was not always without company. A domestic help, who had been employed by the first wife, also worked for the second. In a short while she, too, became aware that something was wrong in the Bennetts' home. She experienced the manifestations which June had encountered, plus one extra: she heard quite clearly her name being called, and recognised the voice as that of the first Mrs Bennett.

Matters continued in this way for several months, and the only member of the household who did not experience any manifestation was the husband. Even the dog sensed something and yapped and whined perpetually.

The charlady finally could not stand the strain of being continually called by her previous employer, and went up to the cemetery to the grave of the departed Mrs Bennett. There she begged the spirit to cease pestering her; but as far as is known the appeal brought no result.

The climax came almost twelve months after June Bennett's arrival in Wroxham. On the couple's return from holiday, June heard both doorbells ring at the same time. She went first to the back, then to the front of the house, but found no one at either door. By this time she was almost inured to the occurrences.

But some nights later a new manifestation occurred, one which could not be shrugged off lightly. June Bennett awoke from sleep to feel something sticky being dragged across her face. She tried to brush away the substance, but it returned. She got out of bed and went downstairs to make herself a drink, and when she returned to bed the sensation did not recur. 'It was,' she said, 'unlike material, but resembled cobwebs, and was certainly sticky.' This appears to have been almost the most anxious and unnerving of the encounters in the Bennetts' house.

Almost, but not quite. The worst manifestation almost certainly was the occasion when June Bennett was seated in front of her dressing-table mirror, putting the final touches to her make-up before going out. As she describes it, the incident occurred thus: 'The mirror,' says Mrs Bennett, 'began to mist over. I tried to wipe it clean, and then saw the reflection in it. It was the face of a woman, but not my face. From my husband's later description, it appears to have been the face of his first wife.' June Bennett did not use that mirror again.

Twelve months exactly after coming to Wroxham, the Bennetts moved into Norwich. The house they had occupied was sold, and the new owners report that it is certainly not haunted now.

Perhaps June Bennett would have forgotten her alarming year at

Wroxham had it not been for a certain bedroom in her new home. This contains all that is left of furniture belonging to her husband's first wife. The charwoman who now works for June reports that the room often has a strange smell. 'Not quite like baking bread, but very near it.'

One could draw various conclusions from this story, though those conclusions must be influenced by what one believes about psychic phenomena. In the case of the Bennetts the fact that the first wife during her life had been possessive regarding her home would suggest that she might be jealous and resentful of a successor. This presupposes that some emotional development is possible after death, and it is necessary to accept this possibility, if the jealousy theory is to be viable. If the developmental theory is unacceptable, then the explanation for the manifestations must be sought elsewhere.

In the opening paragraphs of this book, I wrote: 'Those who have had encounters with the inexplicable are likely to believe in psychic phenomena.' This seems to be the point where the author must declare himself one way or the other. I will say, therefore, that I believe in the existence of phenomena whose manifestation does not conform to the laws of material, terrestrial life. They appear to be extra-terrestrial and therefore not subject to the laws of matter as we understand these at present. By implication, there may be other, as yet undiscovered, laws which in time will provide the coveted 'scientific' explanation for events which appear illogical and apparently chaotic.

I have personally encountered on several occasions such 'extra-terrestrial' occurrences. Two of these encounters took place in Norfolk some years ago. The first occurred in the autumn of 1971. I had moved to Norfolk from Lincolnshire in the January of that year, and had had little time to explore the new countryside. When a friend from my old home came on a week-end visit, it seemed a good opportunity to travel around the nearby village. Therefore on the Saturday afternoon we drove out to the west of Norwich towards the area known as Breckland ('breck' meaning 'heath'). The day was one of the golden October kind belonging to the Indian Summer which certain years produce. The weather was mild, dry and sunny, and the journey a pleasant one. I drove around the villages beyond Colney, until presently the road led into what seemed a particularly pretty hamlet. My friend and I reacted with pleasure to the neat village green, the clump of bronzing trees in its centre, the picturesque cottages encircling it, and to the village church on the farther side of the green. This was the most attractive village we had yet encountered.

I parked my car at the near side of the road encircling the green, which at this point was a good distance away from the trees. Then Mary and I took stock of our surroundings.

We walked the perimeter of the green, and our pleasure in it slowly began to ebb. The cottages, which had seemed a picturesque survival of the past, looked more neglected than we had thought; several of them stood empty, which was extraordinary in view of the general land and house hunger of the times.

We completed our circuit and then one of us, I forget who, suggested that we look at the church. A pleasant enough approach, nothing remarkable about either that or the churchyard. We entered the building, stood for several seconds at the bottom of the nave, and then slowly began to walk up it.

At first, all I felt was a sense of dampness and cold, then I recognised it as something more. There was an oppressive quality in the atmosphere, and whatever the oppression was, grew as the seconds ticked by. I glanced at Mary. She had ceased looking at pews and floor inscriptions and was standing stockstill in the middle of the nave, a frown of concentration on her face. Our eyes caught and flicked away.

She said, 'It's not very pleasant in here, is it?'

It was far from pleasant, and was getting less so every minute.

I said, 'I'm going up to the chancel,' and began to walk towards it. This was less bravery than curiosity. One wished to prove to oneself that the sensation was imaginary; that it would vanish with movement. Instead it grew immediately more concentrated. By the time we stood in the chancel, the sensation of oppression had changed to one of active and evil hostility. It was almost insupportable.

Mary said, 'I can't stand this,' and almost ran down the aisle and out of the building.

I stayed where I was for perhaps two or three minutes, but once she had left, the full force of the concentration seemed focused on me. It was quite impossible to stay in the place, and I hurried out after my friend.

Mary, who was waiting for me outside the church door, asked me what I thought we had encountered, but I had no more idea than she, not knowing the history of the place. All we knew was that we had experienced some malevolent force. The fact that it was in a church apparently made no difference to its power.

By now we were anxious to leave the village, and hurried back to the car. But the inexplicable had occurred there, also. The roof and bonnet of the car were covered with a rash of green spots or droppings, the liquid being of a sticky, glutinous substance. Had it been red one would have concluded it was blood. The drops ran down the windscreen and windows, and were fairly resistant to my attempts to wipe them off.

The trees? They were too far from the car to have caused the trouble. There was no house near; no children who could have played a practical joke. In any case, I have never seen, before or since, any substance of this kind or colour.

My friend's reaction was that of a Norfolk woman born and raised in a mysterious county, who after many years away from it, returns to find conditions unchanged.

'I think it's witchcraft,' Mary said. 'The county has a reputation for it.'

Whatever it was, we left the village at once. Which was a pity in a sense, for it is physically one of the prettiest villages in its area. To this day, I have found no explanation for either of our experiences there.

The second personal *rencontre* arose from researches in connection with this book.

A certain shop in Magdalen Street, Norwich, was formerly part of an old public house (why is it that pubs seem particularly haunt-prone?), which had been sub-divided into several small commercial properties. Radio Rentals, who had previously occupied the premises, moved into newly-developed property in the nearby Anglia Square, and their old shop was taken over by the charity organisation, Oxfam.

Certain members of the staff of the outgoing firm had reason to think the Magdalen Street shop was haunted. A figure had been seen at the foot of a flight of stairs leading to a front room; cold draughts had been felt, etc. The incomers paid little attention of the tales, being too concerned with the organisation of a new business to have time for fantasies. However, once installed, the Oxfam staff were given reason to remember their predecessors' stories.

The large upstairs room at the head of the stairs looks on to Magdalen Street. It is an airy, light, high-ceilinged room, and a short corridor separates its entrance door from the stairhead. The new occupiers made this room into an office, placing a desk diagonally in the left hand side of it. The opposite, right hand, wall is ideal for pinning notices, bulletins, information, etc. These papers were initially fastened to the wall by single long-stemmed pins, about half the length of an old-fashioned hatpin.

Shortly after the new people took over the premises, a number of unusual occurrences were noted: the sound of footsteps mounting the stairs, a feeling of extreme cold in certain parts of the building (particularly the front room previously mentioned), a cold draught moving through this room and the adjacent corridor and stairhead when no windows were open.

These signs were disturbing enough, but worse was to come. Mrs Parry, a secretary in the building, normally works in the front upstairs room. On one occasion while she was in the office, she observed a typewriter apparently working of its own accord, the keys moving regularly; there was also a strong sense of presence in the room and this sensation of not being alone in the office was to be experienced again and again, both by Mrs Parry and by others.

There was enough evidence of psychic disturbance now to warrant calling in a psychical research society, and this was done. The local Press gave the matter some publicity, and the Oxfam staff cut the article and a reproduced

*Magdalen Street, Norwich*

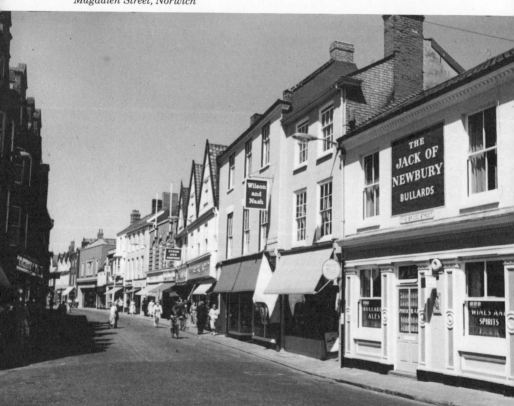

photograph of the proceedings from the newspaper in question. The cutting was fastened to the front office wall with one of the long-stemmed pins previously mentioned.

Shortly afterwards a male member of the staff, Mr Yallop, entered the office and observed that the cutting was swinging backwards and forwards as though in a heavy draught. He could see no reason for the movement. There appeared to be no draught and the room's windows were firmly closed. What is more, other papers pinned to the same wall in a similar fashion were stationary. Only the cutting relating to the haunting swung rhythmically to and fro. Puzzled, Mr Yallop put out his hand and steadied the paper, keeping it quite still for a few minutes. When eventually he released it, the cutting immediately began once more to swing. Although disturbed by the event, the office staff found a practical solution to the problem by using ordinary drawing pins thereafter instead of the long-stemmed variety.

When I called at the shop and asked to see the room reputedly haunted, the premises had already been visited by three separate bodies working in the psychical research field. I understand that all three averred that something extra-terrestrial was present in the building. I made no enquiries into their methods or proofs, for these were outside the scope of my own investigation. Apparently certain recordings had been taken and these had proved to be positive – i.e. had convinced the recorders that psychic phenomena were present.

My reason for visiting was similar to theirs in that I hoped to discover whether the place was truly haunted, but I trusted my own sixth-sense, antennae or animal intuition (one can give this faculty a variety of names) to register the presence or absence of a ghost.

At first I talked downstairs to the staff, and observed a certain amount of tension in the air. However, this seemed natural in view of the considerable publicity which had been given to the matter and the continual visits by sundry interested parties to the shop premises.

Although open-minded on the subject of the ghost's reality, I don't believe I had expected to experience any sensation. I wanted the facts of the story and some sight of the physical background. These were the main reasons for visiting the premises.

Mr Yallop conducted me up the stairs which led to the haunted area and almost immediately I experienced a sensation of physical disturbance. At first mild, it intensified as we climbed the stairs and entered the corridor leading to the front office. By the time the room was reached, the sensation was precise, intense and concentrated. I was not surprised to find it overpoweringly strong in the room itself.

The nature of the physical disturbance which these encounters generate deserves some elaboration. Perhaps it varies from one person to another; I can only describe its effect on myself. It seems to affect first the middle of one's body, the stomach tightens or feels queasy, as in a fear reaction. There is a feeling, also, of *oppression* on the body's surface, as though the atmosphere had acquired additional weight. It is also possible that the body will feel cold, though this I attribute to the drop in air temperature which is common in these cases. It is a sensation of unease and discomfort, though there may be no conscious or active fear apparent in the subject.

This, then, was my physical state on entering and standing in the haunted room. It was at once evident that Mr Yallop and I were not alone in the room. As when one's back is turned to a door and a living person enters noiselessly, one is yet aware that another human being has come into the room. There is a sense of *presence* which is impossible to analyse. I suspect that the recognition of presence is recognition of the concentrated energy contained in a definite and limited form, either human or other.

In this case, the concentration appeared to be in the left hand side of the room and approximately at the far end of the desk. As Mr Yallop and I conversed, it slowly moved from its original position until it was immediately to my left. This, I can assure my readers, was too near for comfort.

During the time we were in the room, my companion was not aware of a sense of presence. I described to him the location of the concentration and he remembered that one of the earlier investigators (a man) had also detected the presence in the same area.

After leaving the room, Mr Yallop told me the alleged story of the haunting. The ghost is said to be that of a woman, a murder victim of late Victorian times. We visited a smaller room in which the murder supposedly took place, but it was almost devoid of sensation. Whatever is in the Oxfam building in Magdalen Street, is in the front upper room.

My impression at the time, and it has remained with me, was that of something imprisoned and desperate to get out. It also seemed to me that there had originally been two low-ceilinged rooms, and that they had been knocked into one and the ceilings raised when modernisation took place.

This is purely surmise, but if correct, would account for the ghost's presence in one half of the room rather than the other. Ghosts appear to be firmly fixed in their own time and the physical circumstances of that time. If a door habitually used during life is subsequently bricked up, the ghost continues to walk through the place where the door has been, thus appearing to walk through the wall. This frequently causes more distress to the onlooker than to the ghost, who is unaware that the doorway has gone.

Time certainly seems to be a strongly operative element in psychic manifestations. I hope to return later to this aspect of hauntings.

As I write, investigations of the Magdalen Street ghost are still being carried out, and there has been some talk of using exorcism. With a presence so strong, exorcism may not be enough.

All reputedly haunted buildings have not this sense of presence. A stately Elizabethan house, known as Curat House, in the centre of Norwich is said to be haunted by the spirit of a Mr Isaacs, a former rabbi. In medieval times this area of the city was part of the Jewish quarter, and the area contained the synagogue, schools and houses of the community. Fire destroyed the district between 1286 and 1291, and the present building was erected between 1480 and 1501 by John Curat, who later became one of the two Norwich sheriffs. The Tudor house was commemoratively known as 'Old Jewry'. Following Curat's death, the house eventually became the property of the Back family during the reign of Charles II and has been occupied by members of this family until its sale in 1971 to a national firm of men's outfitters. During the Back's occupation, the premises were used first as a grocer's and chandler's, and later as a wine merchant's.

About the year 1889, the wine trade had grown to such an extent that the cellars of the premises had to be rebuilt to accommodate extra stock. In the course of this work stone columns were discovered in the basement, together with items of glass and pottery. It was concluded at the time that the basement of Old Jewry concealed the crypt of the original synagogue; a stratum of burnt earth seemed to bear out this theory. But pottery was not the only item to be discovered in the excavations. The bones of a woman were also disturbed – a Mrs Isaacs, said to have been murdered by her husband and buried there. Isaacs is also believed to have been responsible for the burning of the synagogue, though no motive has come to light for this activity.

Since the time of the excavations, however, Curat House has apparently been haunted by the spirit of the remorseful Isaacs. Footsteps have been heard (usually during the third week in November) walking upstairs, along the gallery and past what was once the main bedroom of the house.

Colonel Philip Back, a wonderfully alert old gentleman of over ninety summers, told me that he clearly remembers his father calling out 'Who's there?', and on investigating, finding no author of the footsteps. The Backs kept a staff of servants, and all had been alarmed by sounds of someone walking about, climbing the stairs to the servants' quarters. The family had difficulty in keeping maids on account of these disturbances. Philip Back, himself, however, had never heard the ghost.

When I visited the premises with Colonel Back, the builders were again in occupation and the ground floor of the fine Tudor building had been gutted to prepare it for its new role as a gentleman's outfitters. The old bedroom was reasonably intact, though wainscoting, great fireplace, and beamed ceiling were grey with the excavators' dust. I stood at the head of the stairs, alert for some sign of an uneasy presence. It was again the third week in November, but the house was desolate, empty save for us two and the numerous builders, whistling and calling to each other as they carried on their work in the shell.

Whatever walked in Curat House appears to do so no longer. The destruction of his material surroundings may have laid Isaacs's wandering spirit. No doubt time will prove or disprove that theory. I shall await reactions from the outfitters' staff with interest.

One of the better-known and most widely publicised of Norfolk ghosts is that at Snettisham, a detailed history of which is given by the Rev. R. W. Maitland in a Psychic Press publication. The following story has no obvious connection with the Maitland account, as far as I can tell, though it may be significant that the locality (the village of Snettisham) is the same in both cases. Maitland's story, however, is concerned with Cobb Hall or Park House; Mr Harvey's* story relates to the actual vicarage at Snettisham.

In April 1965 a new incumbent moved into Snettisham vicarage. The Rev. Harvey and his family had previously lived in the Isle of Man and had two grown up sons, Stephen and Graham, aged respectively twenty and sixteen at the time of the new appointment. The younger son, Graham, was still at school on the island and during his first holidays at Snettisham noticed that his parents seemed uneasy, though the boy could not fathom the cause.

A week after his arrival, however, he encountered the first of a series of strange happenings. At around 1.00 a.m., as he was about to get into bed, he heard footsteps in the corridor outside his room. His parents' room being farther along the same corridor, he assumed that one of them was responsible for the footsteps. A few seconds elapsed, then he heard his father call out, 'Is that you, Graham?' The boy replied in the negative, and both father and son then went into the corridor and turned on the light. The corridor was silent and empty.

For Graham this was the first of many occasions of hearing footsteps in the house. At various times through the years, all the Harvey family heard these unexplained sounds. The elder son, Stephen, who had been working on the Isle of Man, moved to Snettisham, and his letters to his schoolboy brother soon began to mention the odd happenings at the vicarage. The noises were always heard at night at around 1.00 a.m. and frequently when there were guests in the house. The feeling of agitation and disturbance began seriously to unsettle the family. Mrs Harvey, who at 51 had appeared much less than her age, now found her hair turning grey. Although far from 'imaginative' people, the family were showing the strain of living in this house.

During the next two years, a series of inexplicable occurrences took place; knockings were heard upon doors, shadows crossed the ceilings and various bumps and bangings were heard throughout the house.

The fact that Mr Harvey was a clergyman made it difficult for him to discuss the state of affairs with anyone outside his own family, although one friend who had been associated with spiritualism remarked on the uneasy atmosphere of the house and chose to sleep at the local inn rather than stay there.

One particularly gruesome manifestation occurred when the two brothers were sharing a room. Guests were staying with the Harveys at the time, and the boys were required to double up in one room in order to provide better accommodation for one of the visitors.

They were sharing one of the two small rooms which appear mainly to have been associated with the haunting. The lads had talked until very late, and the time was about one o'clock in the morning, when without warning they heard the sound of a human heartbeat in the room – very loud, much magnified but unmistakably the double thump of a beating heart. Understandably, they were petrified, but as soon as movement was possible, they fled from the room and spent the night in another.

When approached, the previous vicar stated that he had heard 'birds under the floorboards'. The present vicar, who succeeded Mr Harvey, has apparently heard nothing and been told nothing of the mysterious goings-on.

If the vicarage is no longer haunted, it may be because certain structural alterations to the house have been made by the present incumbent. Walls in the two small rooms where the hauntings mainly occurred have been removed. This may be one more instance of a disturbance of material surroundings affecting the positive nature of a manifestation.

Whether there is any connection between the disturbances at the vicarage and the more famous Snettisham ghost originating at Cobb Hall, it is impossible to tell. The Harvey family can vouch for their own experiences, even though they know of no explanation, either in past or recent history. This must remain another record of haunting by person or persons unknown.

Another story of a different but equally mysterious nature was told me by Bryan Hall of Banningham Rectory.

Mr Hall is the possessor of two items reputed to be haunted. The first is a portrait of a Miss Henrietta Nelson, who died at Yaxley Hall in Suffolk on 4 April 1815. Miss Nelson had been brought up at the Hall, but had occupied an inferior position as she was, unfortunately for her, illegitimate. The nineteenth century regarded bastardy to the shame of the child as much as of its parents, and the proud and sensitive Miss Nelson no doubt suffered accordingly. One glance at that face is enough to convince of its owner's resentment at patronage from luckier members of her family.

Whatever Henrietta felt during her lifetime, she expressed a strong wish that on her death she should not be buried in the family vault at Yaxley, but should occupy a mausoleum in the Hall grounds.

Her end came abruptly. She fell down a short flight of stairs from her

*Miss Henrietta Nelson*

bedroom and died as a result of the fall. She was buried, as she had requested, in the vault in the grounds. Apparently it was a very expensive vault, and lay near the path through the park to the church. This was precisely as the lady had requested, and all went well for many years afterwards. In fact, until the middle of the century, when a new owner came into possession of the Hall. Knowing nothing of the mauseoleum's history, he found it inconvenient to leave it in the situation in which he found it. He removed Miss Nelson's remains to the family vault, and demolished her burial place. Shortly afterwards the form of Miss Nelson began to be seen in the grounds of Yaxley Hall.

In the course of time, the ghost came to be associated with Miss Nelson's picture, and wherever the picture hung there the ghost appeared.

The painting eventually left Yaxley and was owned by a family living at Barton Turf, between Wroxham and Stalham. There Miss Nelson was seen by the portrait's present owner, Mr Bryan Hall. As he approached the house he saw the unmistakable face of Henrietta Nelson at the north bedroom window, looking out towards the churchyard.

Mr Hall had a similar experience at Smallburgh. He saw Miss Nelson standing in the old kitchen courtyard (since pulled down); she was looking into the kitchen window, and he recognised her without difficulty because of her resemblance in face and dress to her portrait.

The next time he saw her was in the same house. She stood on the lower landing, framed in a doorway. The apparition gave no impression of colour, apart from a parchment-like quality of the face.

Mr Hall now owns Miss Nelson's portrait. He told me, before we went into the sitting-room to see it, that she has never been seen at Banningham, though visitors have sensed her presence there.

My own experience of this picture was an odd one. On first arriving at the Rectory, Mr Hall showed me into the drawing-room, and I stood six feet from Henrietta Nelson's portrait and regarded it. Or did she regard me? Her brows were drawn together, her mouth pulled down. Never have I seen a woman's face portray disapproval and hostility so acutely. I felt discomfited enough to be glad to retreat into another room to hear the main story of the haunting.

Afterwards something in her story touched me, and I said so to my host. 'Poor old thing. It must have been hard for a woman like her to be illegitimate in those days.' No more than that was said; a simple expression of sympathy.

When I looked at the portrait once again on leaving the Rectory, I was so astounded I stood with my mouth open for a few minutes. *The whole expression of the picture had changed.* Gone were the frown, the tight lips, the disapproving glare. Miss Henrietta Nelson was almost smiling. 'What a kind old face' you would have said.

Bryan Hall was amused at my astonishment. 'She does this sometimes,' he said. 'Many people have remarked on it.' It wasn't even a trick of the light, for there was no sun to throw shadows. Something about the technique of the painting perhaps? Mr Hall did not know. 'Her expression changes,' he said, 'often in a matter of minutes.'

If the story of the portrait is strange that of the chair is even stranger.

This particular chair stands in the centre of the same room which houses Henrietta Nelson's portrait. It is an ordinary piece of early-nineteenth-century furniture, rather drab, rather shabby, nothing remarkable about it save a certain delicacy of shape typical of the period.

The chair was formerly owned by Mrs Mary Hutt, widow of Canon H. R. M.

Hutt, who was sometime Rector of Bingham in Nottinghamshire. After her widowhood she came to live at Dilham, where Mr Hall's father was vicar, and it was then that Mr Hall met her and first set eyes on the chair. When he remarked upon it, she told him the following curious story.

Shortly after the First World War when the Hutts were living at Bingham Rectory, Mrs Hutt had occasion to go to Nottingham with her chauffeur. As she was to visit the dentist and afterwards to complete her shopping, she made an arrangement to meet the man later in the day. She had completed the first part of her assignment, and was bent on shopping, when she was caught in a terrific thunderstorm and forced to take shelter in a hurry. She turned down a side street and took refuge in the first shop she saw, standing in the doorway while the rain and thunder obliterated the afternoon street.

It was at that moment that she heard a voice behind her cry 'Save me! Save me!' She spun round and looked into the shop for the first time.

It was a poor sort of antique shop, one which nowadays would be called a junk shop. The interior was murky after the outside light, but she could make out a chair in one corner. In it sat a woman wearing (to quote Mrs Hutt's own words) 'a sumptuous dress'. The lady had red hair, and to judge by her expression a violent temper. Mrs Hutt took a pace into the shop, but the apparition did not vanish, merely reiterated, 'Save me! Save me!'

Before Mrs Hutt could decide what she should do, the shop's proprietor emerged from a back room. Somewhat shaken by this time, Mrs Hutt stammered that she had only come in to shelter from the rain. She turned back to the chair then, but saw it was empty.

Feeling that she should buy something, she chose the chair and purchased it for a few shillings. The information that it had come from Newstead Abbey meant little to her at the time.

By this time the storm had abated, so she left the shop and on meeting the chauffeur, sent him back for the chair.

The journey home was remarkable for the odd behaviour of the car, which began to weave across the road, causing the chauffeur to think the steering was at fault; however, there had been no such problem on the journey into Nottingham.

On reaching home the chair was taken out and put in the servants' hall for the night and Jane, one of the maids, was given instructions to scrub it with soap and water the next morning.

However, while Mrs Hutt was attending to correspondence in the drawing-room after breakfast, the girl Jane knocked at the door and said she was unable to scrub the new chair as she thought it was bewitched. Mrs Hutt then agreed to wash the object herself.

What happened at this point Mr Hall was unable to tell me in detail, beyond the fact that whenever the chair was placed near a firegrate – whether or not the fire was alight – the woman Mrs Hutt had first seen reappeared seated in it.

Now its owner decided that the chair had better be kept away from the fire if the Rectory's inhabitants were to have any peace, and from that time on it was placed as far as possible from a fireplace. On one or two occasions when it was accidentally moved near to a fire, the ghostly lady at once appeared.

When Mrs Hutt's husband died, she moved into a rented house in Norfolk, and the first day after she had moved in she went into the drawing-room, with her small dog following at her heels. The place was as chaotic as houses usually are the day after a move, and furniture was everywhere. She did not therefore find it surprising when her little dog showed signs of great excitement, flying to the window and barking furiously. His mistress, who had been putting linen covers on the chairs, stopped what she was doing to see what was the cause of the animal's agitation. She looked out of the window and saw coming up the drive the lady she had seen in the antique shop. She looked round then for the haunted chair. It was standing in the fireplace where it had been left by one of the removal men. Mrs Hutt was not surprised when the lady came into the room and sat in her chair.

When Mrs Hutt in turn died, she left the chair to Bryan Hall – but only on condition that he never experimented with it by placing it near a fire. He was pleased to have the piece and was not tempted to flout his old friend's wishes.

It was the chair which played the last card in the game, however. On hearing that the piece of furniture was his, Mr Hall arranged with the village postmaster to collect it in the latter's car. The chair was placed in the back seat, but all the way to its destination the car's steering gave trouble.

Mr Hall has honoured his promise and the chair has never again been placed near a fire, nor, as far as I am aware at the time of writing, has the lady reappeared to cry 'Save me! Save me!'

Who was she, the woman of the sumptuous dress and the violent temper? And why is the proximity of fire the catalyst to her appearance? The chair, you will remember, came from Newstead Abbey, once the home of Lord Byron. The lady may have been of his family.

But 'Save me! Save me!' – and the significance of fire; was there, I wondered, ever a great conflagration at Newstead?

The answer came more quickly than I expected. Margaret Morris, the friend whose own ghost story I have told in another chapter, was brought up in the village of Newstead, and knew something of the Abbey's history.

'Yes,' she said, when I asked her. 'There certainly was a fire at the Abbey, and much of the building was destroyed.' She did not know the date, however, or whether any life had been lost in the disaster.

Was the lady burned to death? What else could have been meant by her cry for help? What else could be the significance of fire, which brought her back to the chair she had used in life? One loses one's way in a maze of guesses and surmises, which, fascinating though they are, bring the investigator no nearer to certainty of the truth. Some day I intend to learn the story of the fire at Newstead Abbey, and not I think until then shall I understand the story of the lady in the painted chair.

There are many other recorded hauntings in Norfolk. A man on a black horse is reputed to ride the neighbourhood of Ranworth Broad, and the ghostly black dog of Celtic legend has been seen several times along the east coast of the county. In Norfolk this phantom animal is known as 'Old Shuck', though in other parts of England he has other names, the best known being that of the trash or padfoot. Occasionally the legendary dog is white, as at Cawthorpe in Lincolnshire. I suspect that in cases where a similar ghost appears in many widely-scattered areas, the apparition is not an echo of a life once lived on earth, but is a racial or archetypal memory, perhaps of a one-time religious fetish or object of reverence in pagan days. Certainly the padfoot reaches right back in time – as far, at least, as the Scottish kelpie or the Irish banshee. Such visual creations are planted deep in the imagination of the race, handed down hereditarily in some part of the unconscious mind in a manner not yet understood. At what point the memory derived from actual event, it is impossible to tell. There are many buried facts which the race rather than the individual remembers. Giants and dragons, for instance, now thought to be imaginative creations, may at one time have been realities for our remote ancestors.

So, perhaps, with the padfoot, 'Old Shuck'. A giant dog, with staring eyes. The earliest known horses were about the size of giant dogs. An idea, only, I await a better one.

One last story from Norfolk remains to be told. It is related of Old Catton, which is two miles as the crow flies from my home. The ghost is that of a familiar Woman in White – said to be a daughter of the local Manor House. The tale goes that the lady loved one of her father's coachmen, who resided in a lodge on the opposite side of the lane from the big house, and nightly stole out to visit him. Why she should return to act out her innocent guilt heaven knows, but the white-clad girl has been seen on several occasions crossing and recrossing the road now known as White Woman Lane.

In another ancient house in Catton village, a male ghost has been seen and (rather more often) heard. Footsteps, banging doors and all the usual accompaniments of manifestation have occurred; and a man has been seen standing by the sink in the kitchen of the ground-floor flat. Apparently the presence is not unfriendly, for residents continue to occupy the building without complaint.

*Old Catton Village*

# LINCOLNSHIRE
## Walking Boots and Pigs and a Spanish Noblewoman

Lincolnshire is not, as popular opinion supposes, a large county composed entirely of flat fertile acres, where the eye can see an uninterrupted view for twenty miles or more. True, the southern division of Holland, and to some extent the south of the middle division of Kesteven are wide, flat and open for miles to the searching fingers of the east wind, but in the north of the county matters are differently arranged. Drive north from Boston to Horncastle and you cover mile after mile of monotonous near-sea-level arable land; but once past Horncastle you climb up into the Wolds and are immediately in beautiful rolling hill-country with great fields patterning the hillsides, and little copses crowning the Wold-tops, neat farms tucked here and there between.

It is an ancient countryside. The south of the county was once fenland and knew the old wildfowlers who crept up and down the waterways in their punts after geese, duck, plover or any other winged creature they could cook and eat. To the west lie the lands associated with the Pilgrim Fathers, where the first Dissenting congregations met to worship; lands over which they travelled in a persistent attempt to escape religious persecution, until finally they were driven to leave their native country entirely. In Lindsey in the north lies the area associated with the Pilgrimage of Grace, whose rebellious members caused Henry VIII to refer to Lincolnshire as 'that brute and bestiale county'. The rebels, objecting to the dissolution of their monasteries, made their displeasure felt in tangible fashion by beating and imprisoning the King's representatives and burning His Majesty's decree of Dissolution. Henry's reprisal, like his temper, was quick, hot and terrifying. The rebellion came to an abrupt end, as did the lives of some of its participants.

The eastern lands of Lincolnshire are coast lands – flat sea-marshes, where the wild geese feed in autumn and winter, or mudflats which stretch along the tideline, providing food for the countless waders – sanderlings, oyster-catchers, knots, turnstones, curlews – which haunt the area.

It is a strange and beautiful county, perhaps the least known and appreciated in East Anglia, certainly less frequented than Norfolk or Suffolk, less on the main traffic routes than Hertfordshire or Northampton-shire. But once find it and it lays its charm on you for life.

Inevitable that it should have its stories of hauntings and ghosts. Many of these are concerned with historical incidents or personages rather than with the personal family patterns which are common in Norfolk.

An interesting story was recently told me by Miss Joyce Lucas of Lincoln, concerning an experience of her father's.

In his youth, Mr Lucas worked in the neighbourhood of Cammeringham, a small village on the B1398 road, between Brattleby and Ingham near the old Roman Ermine Street. He was an early riser, and in fact needed to be so, since he began work shortly after daybreak.

Mr Lucas was walking to work one morning just as dawn was breaking. It was a misty start to the day, and the vapour was formed in banks and patches as it sometimes is when heat is promised later. The sun was rising, however, and the day grew brighter as the man walked. Without realising it, Mr Lucas focused his attention on a particularly large bank of mist which was drifting towards him. As it drew nearer there emerged from it a chariot driven by a woman and pulled by two horses, one white, one black. The woman's dress was long and loosely flowing; her hair also lay loose over her shoulders. She whipped the horses, and as she moved, the early sunlight caught and lit a quantity of gold jewellery which she wore. Within seconds the chariot was again swallowed up in the mist. Throughout the occurrence there had been no sound of any kind.

This apparition has been seen on several occasions over the centuries, and is known locally as 'The Cammeringham Light'. Mr Lucas was of the firm opinion that he had seen Queen Boadicea, and this is a fairly viable explanation since the territory of the Iceni, over which tribe Boadicea ruled, bordered what is now southern Lincolnshire. It is conceivable that the Queen might travel the few miles farther north, also that she would make use of the nearby Roman road.

Another and much later apparition is connected with the same area.

During the Second World War, Lincolnshire became one giant airfield, supplying bomber and fighter squadrons for offence and defence against Nazi Germany. A group of bomber stations was clustered around Lincoln itself, and one, Scampton, earned individual fame as the base for the noted 'Dam Buster' raiders.

I lived in Lincoln myself during the war, and each night heard the drone of laden bombers labouring into the sky and lay awake in the early hours, ears a-strain for the sound of their return. Sometimes on the outward flight they did not make take-off, and then the city and countryside around would be shaken by a huge and horrible detonation as plane and bombs exploded.

But more often the crashes were on the return journey – planes limping in with part of the fuselage shot away, or with half the crew dead or injured. Often one could tell by the mere sound that they were in trouble, and then one prayed for them without daring to get out of bed and look.

Towards the end of the war a curious story became current in Lincoln and the surrounding area, and Miss Lucas, after speaking of her father's experience, reminded me of the wartime tale.

A bomber was returning to Scampton after a particularly bad raid over Germany. The aircraft had been hit by flak and damaged sufficiently to make it unlikely that it would get back to base. The plane had become difficult to navigate and the crew, now in bad shape, had no idea where they were.

Night flights in winter can be unpleasant even in peace time. In time of war, with a damaged aircraft and injured crew, snow-covered fields rushing up to meet you are not a reassuring sight. The pilot looked out desperately for some reasonable-looking field where he could get the plane down. At last he saw what he needed, and with skill and luck, managed to land the damaged aircraft safely. But the crew needed help. They needed above all to find their home airfield. In the middle of a snowy winter's night that was a pretty hopeless expectation: the snow obliterated all landmarks.

Had they known it, they were only a mile or so from Scampton itself, and a few hundred yards from the main road. But everything looked alike, a wilderness of black and white with no guidelines. How could they know where they were or in which direction to go?

The need was so urgent, however, that one of the men decided to try to find his way to a road in the hope of securing help. He left the aircraft and set out, stumbling across the fields and dykes. He found neither road nor help, but walked in circles, gradually growing weaker. He was about to turn back to try to return to the aircraft, when the figure of a man appeared ahead and beckoned to him. He was relieved to see the farmhand and only too glad to follow where the person led. In a short while they reached the main road, and the airman turned round to thank his guide. The figure had disappeared.

Later, enquiries were made to see if any farmworkers or local people had been in the area at the time, and it appeared that none had. The airman had seen either a ghost or some other supernatural manifestation.

This story has much in common with the 'Angels of Mons' legend of the First World War. Men in extreme danger seeking help or reassurance are afforded it by supernatural means. I have not met any person who experienced this phenomenon at first-hand, nor yet spoken to anyone who knew a member of the aircrew concerned. This must be accepted as a 'miracle' tale, I think, rather than a ghost story in the usual sense of that term.

There are many ghost stories of a more conventional nature in the county, several of them associated with the rural life which is typical of an agricultural area. One such was told me by a farming friend. It concerns a farm at Wold Newton, not far from Grimsby, where the hills begin to smooth down towards the sea. It is still picturesque scenery, and the villages in the area were founded centuries ago, some in Saxon or Danish times, for this was heavily invaded land. This particular farm had been established since the eighteenth century, and retained intact its original barn although a modern one had been built near it and was used in place of the old.

I have not found a record of the first manifestations, but for many years now the old barn has been a place to avoid at harvest time. Local people aver that on late August evenings the building is lit up, faintly and with flickering light, by many candles; and if you go near enough the sound of flails can be heard, threshing out the grain. The noise of flails is a long forgotten one, but hear it once and you would not mistake it for anything else. The old men of Wold Newton know quite well what is taking place in the ancient barn, and you would not get them within a mile of it at harvest time.

Not far away across the Wold-tops lies Binbrook, once a thriving little town, but now a large village whose claim to distinction is the possession of an RAF station on its doorstep.

It is a charming, sleepy village, with a broad main street, into which run roads from Market Rasen, Louth and Grimsby, among others. A mellow and ageing manor house graces one side of the street, owned by Brigadier Clarke, to whom I am indebted for the following story.

Binbrook was one of the villages concerned in the Pilgrimage of Grace, but one hundred years later it heard the march of soldiers' feet again when the Royalist and Parliamentary forces clashed at Winceby near Horncastle. Winceby is a considerable distance as the crow flies from Binbrook, being south-south-east of that village by some twenty miles. Yet the latter could well have been a gathering point for armed men if not an actual camp, for it was well-stocked with grain and livestock.

The story goes that a woman walking along the verge of a road out of the village saw coming towards her three soldiers in full uniform. She registered the fact with some surprise. What were soldiers doing here? Airmen she could have understood, for they would have been personnel from the nearby Air Force station. But soldiers – and in armour . . . ! *Armour?* As her mind registered this fact she looked up again, but there were no soldiers to be seen. They had, she recollected, been wearing metal breast-plates and round steel caps. I believe I am correct in thinking that round cap-helmets of the kind she described have only been worn at one period by English soldiers – during the Civil Wars, by Cromwell's Ironsides, the 'Roundheads'.

Why should three Roundheads be walking along a country road, miles from the nearest battlefield? And why should this event so have imprinted itself on its surroundings that the image continued to appear three hundred years later? There is as yet no answer to these questions.

My own home town is a scant ten miles from Binbrook and lies at the foot of the Wolds facing seawards, though the sea itself is a further eight miles away at its nearest point. Louth is a lively market town in the middle of a large agricultural area. I was born there, went to school there (as did the poet, Tennyson, a hundred and twenty years earlier), and spent a large part of my life in the little town.

When I was eleven my family moved to a new house. It was new in the sense that it had been built for them, but it and the two houses to its left were all constructed on the site of a much earlier dwelling. This had been an early Victorian mansion surrounded by a considerable garden. Our house, which was in fact a large bungalow, was built exactly over the foundations of the old house, while the remaining two dwellings – the builder, an artistic fellow, referred to them as 'villas' – stood in what had formerly been the garden of the original structure.

The bungalow was a neat place with two reception rooms either side the entrance hall, and a long corridor dividing off the reception areas from the bedrooms. The hall and this corridor formed a T-shape, with the corridor as its crossbar. We lived in it for forty years and experienced life's usual vicissitudes there.

Most of the time there was nothing remarkable about the house; only occasionally an incident would occur which was puzzling. One would be walking down the corridor which bisected the house when a sudden impulse would cause one to step aside – to allow someone else to pass by. There was no conscious decision to move aside; only the instinctive reaction felt when two people approach along a passageway wide enough for only one. In turn every member of my family made that instinctive movement; and not once, but many times.

There were other inexplicable incidents. The back door carried a brass knocker moulded in the form of the Lincoln Imp. It was an unremarkable object and stiff to operate. It needed a deliberate movement to lift and knock; in other words, once lifted the knocker did not fall by its own weight, but required some applied manual force. Yet many times, both night and day, that knocker has rapped on the back door, and some luckless member of the family has answered to no caller. At first it was unnerving but after a while one ceased to notice it.

There was one occasion, however, when the knocker did not go unremarked.

My mother had been seriously ill for some days, and my father, sister and myself were in a state of anxiety and tension. We were expecting hourly to be summoned to the hospital and were dreading what news that summons might contain.

It happened on a Wednesday night, some time just after midnight. My sister was sleeping in the single upstairs bedroom which the bungalow possessed. She was awakened by the sound of the back door knocker being smartly rapped. She had lived in that house less than the rest of the family, and it did not occur to her to think that this was not a flesh-and-blood summons. She ran downstairs, flung open the back door, and found no one there. She immediately ran into the dining-room, whose window faced into the gravelled road in which we lived. For a moment she could see nothing save the gate at the top of the flight of steps which led down into the road. Then she saw a tall figure wearing dark or black garments descending the steps. It turned left into the roadway and walked along until it reached a similar flight of steps leading to the next door house. It turned to climb these and disappeared from view. Five hours later my mother died.

On enquiry of the neighbour later, we learned without surprise that no one had visited their home in the early hours of that Wednesday morning.

Throughout the time we lived in that house, we rarely thought of explanations for the occasional strange occurrences. The atmosphere of the place was a pleasant one – certainly not 'haunted' or uncomfortable. But it *was* built on the site of an older structure; and who is to say what manner of house the original was?

Louth's history is ancient enough to make its liability to hauntings unsurprising; there are, in fact, fewer such occurrences than one would expect in a town which was the starting point of the Pilgrimage of Grace, which saw the fighting Royalist and Parliamentary forces, and which hid six Saxon graves under its market place until as late as the nineteenth century, when they were discovered and removed.

One story of remarkable charm and power has spread its legend over the centuries and indeed at one time was well enough known throughout England to cause a song to be written in its honour.

It concerns the small Tudor mansion of Thorpe Hall, situated on the main road westward out of Louth. It is a compact squire's house, the main part of which is built at right angles to the road, though some servants' quarters follow the high wall which bounds the area of gardens surrounding the dwelling.

The road which runs by the house goes to Lincoln, Elkington and Market Rasen, and is known as the Elkington Road. On one side the high wall guards it, on the other side, even higher trees, which arch across and in places meet with the other trees growing within the Thorpe Hall grounds. At all times of the year the avenue is shadowed and a little mysterious, but particularly so in summer.

Was it summer when she first came here, the Spanish lady, wearing her green silk dress, which billowed in the wind as she walked? Was it summer when she died at the foot of a tree in Thorpe Hall gardens? We cannot know the facts now, though the Green Lady has been seen many times over the centuries, walking in the Hall grounds, or crossing the road which leads to Elkington.

These are several versions of the story, but the one which has the greatest ring of truth runs as follows.

During Elizabethan times when Britain and Spain fought a series of declared and undeclared wars, the then owner of Thorpe Hall, Sir John Bolle, was captured while fighting the Spaniards and imprisoned in a Spanish dungeon. The window of his cell, however, was above ground, and a certain beautiful Spanish noblewoman regularly passed by it. After a while she stopped to speak with the prisoner, then later she brought him food. It was not long before she found herself hopelessly in love with the Englishman.

Her passion for him was great enough for her to run serious risks on his behalf. She bribed, it is said, his jailers with some of her jewels, and when she had secured Sir John's freedom, she gave him the remaining jewels to enable him to return to England. She made only one request in return: that she be

*Thorpe Hall, Louth*

allowed to accompany John Bolle back to his own country. Bolle, however, was happily married, and could not accede to the request. The lady relinquished him; but not for long. Unable to live without her love, she followed him to England and arrived at Thorpe Hall wearing her most beautiful dress of green silk. She walked up the long garden of the house in the gathering dusk, drawn by the lighted windows and the sounds of laughter.

When she was near enough to see, she perceived the man she loved, seated with his wife and children at the candlelit dinner-table. She had no place there.

Unable to bear either their happiness or her own grief, the lady stabbed herself at the foot of an oak tree in the garden and died.

She has been seen many times, at least twice within my own memory. On one occasion a cyclist from a nearby village saw her walk in front of him. He fell off his bicycle trying to avoid the woman, but when he picked himself up, fully prepared to give her a piece of his mind for jay-walking, the lady was not to be seen.

On the second occasion some time in the 1930s, the then Vicar of Elkington was driving along the road on his way home. A heavy downpour of rain almost obliterated his vision, and the windscreen-wipers had difficulty coping with the volume of water. It was dark, cold and wet and he was anxious to be home by his log fire.

He was driving past the high wall when he saw her, a woman dressed in green, walking in the middle of the road ahead of his car. He was about to wind down the window to call to her, when he noticed her dress; it was billowing out behind her as though in a summer breeze; and it was perfectly dry. On that moment of realisation, he looked again at the figure, but the roadway was empty. Only the driving rain and he in his rain-soaked car were on that piece of roadway.

During the last war, soldiers were billeted in Thorpe Hall. I do not know what they saw or heard, though I am told that occasionally a figure was seen to move through an open doorway. However it was, they carried on a tradition at the Hall as old as the legend itself; they laid an extra place at table each night for the Spanish lady.

She has not been seen for several years now, so perhaps the vibrations of that distant tragedy are growing weak. Occasionally one still hears the song (sung perhaps by a knowledgeable group of folk-singers) which is called *The Spanish Lady*.

> Have you seen the Spanish Lady
> How she loved an Englishman?

My grandfather knew people who had seen her, but that was around the turn of the century. These manifestations grow less powerful with the passing of time, and eventually seem to die away altogether.

This is Louth's great ghost story, of course, but there are other, minor visitations which go unremarked in the town.

One such occurs in the house of Mr John Bourne. Mr Bourne is a considerable antiquarian and historian and has afforded me much help in the past during my researches. His house is, as far as I recollect, seventeenth century mainly, though built on earlier foundations. The back premises and outbuildings are certainly older, though the backyard contains a mounting-block once used by Lord Byron on a visit to the then owners of the house.

Within the house a staircase sweeps up from the hall to the upper floors. On one occasion, the Bournes heard the sound of footsteps running swiftly down the staircase, then abruptly ceasing in the hall. At the foot of the stairs on the right are two doors, one leading into the dining-room and that beyond it to a cellar, always now kept locked.

On hearing the sound of running, Mr Bourne had assumed that an intruder had broken into his home. He went to the hearth, picked up a poker, then hurried into the hall to deal with whoever had illicitly entered it. The hall was empty.

Perhaps he was not entirely surprised, for he knew the story of that staircase and hallway.

It seems that about 1880 a woman who had then lived in the house had been late for dinner, had run down the stairs at speed and turned right into what she thought was the dining-room. In the darkness she mistook the door, and entered the second not the first door she came to. In those days the cellar door was not locked. She fell headlong down the twenty steps, breaking her neck in the fall. The Bournes are convinced they heard a re-enactment of the woman's last living moments, and she may have repeated many times the events of that particular night. I use the term 'she', though I am by no means satisfied that what appears to be human or a reflection or refraction of human presence is actually so. I believe that what the eye sees or the ear hears is an *imprint* of a former event or person. Too early, however, to come to conclusions about this yet. Let me tell you instead of another Louth spectre.

For several years my mother employed a domestic help, whose husband was, among other things, a competent carpenter. On one occasion he was required to do a minor job of this nature in a house near the church.

I say 'the church' as though the town had only one. In fact it has three Anglican churches, but the only one referred to so intimately is the great parish church of St James, which dominates not only the town of Louth, but the countryside for a ten-mile radius around. The building was completed in 1515, and possesses the third highest spire in England. Every structure near by is dwarfed by it, including the cluster of elderly houses at its feet, known as Church Close. They are mainly Georgian houses with occasional Victorian additions. In one of these our charwoman's husband was required to do a simple job of repairing a damaged window sash in one of the attic bedrooms. It would take less than an hour he thought to complete the work.

When he reached the place, however, he found the damage more extensive than he had thought and requiring more time to repair. There was little furniture in the room – a single bed, a chair and not much else. He put his tools on the chair, and worked away at the broken window sash. After half an hour he heard someone enter the room behind him. Thinking it was the lady of the house, and being intent on his work at the window, he spoke over his shoulder without turning.

'Sorry I'm taking so long, lady. There was more to do than I thought.'

He waited for the reply, but when it failed to come he looked round. He saw seated on the bed a young, pretty girl wearing a long dark dress, with a frilled apron and a small white cap perched on her dark hair. Dangling from the back of the cap were long strings or streamers. He looked at her in some surprise, for he was not aware that there was a servant in the house. For a moment he turned back to his work, then said again, 'I shan't be much longer. Nearly finished now.' This time the lack of an answer struck him as odd, and he turned round sharply to look at the girl. The room was empty, the door was shut. There was no mark on the bed to show that anyone had been sitting there. The man was certain then that he had not seen a flesh-and-blood woman. He finished the job as rapidly as he could and left the house at once. No explanation for this sighting has even been proffered, and I know of no other person who has encountered this Victorian maidservant, if this is what she was. No doubt in life the room had been hers and she had left enough of herself in it for the imprint to be picked up at a later date by a sensitive subject.

In an agricultural area it is inevitable that many ghost stories should concern farms. One such was told to me by a friend who is herself a farmer's wife. Hazel and Ernest Willows, in their early married life, lived in a farm at East Stockwith, near Gainsborough, and Ernie Willow's family had owned the place for two hundred years. It was traditionally constructed, with a square crewyard flanked by stables and outbuildings and the farmhouse a little distance away.

One pleasant September evening, Hazel went across to the crew, intending to tell her husband that his supper was ready, for she knew that at that time Ernie would be in the stables feeding the horses. As she approached the crewyard, she perceived an old man leaning against the side of the stables. She did not remember having seen him about the farm previously, and noticed his appearance particularly. He was small, stout, wearing fawn coloured breeches, leggings and a checked coat; on his head was a hard, pork-pie type of hat. She remembers clearly that his dress did not appear to be modern.

Hazel called to him. He did not reply, but merely looked at her, then turned and went into the stable. She ran after him, but when she entered the stable it was empty. She told her husband about the incident and described in detail the little old man she had seen. 'That,' Ernie Willows said, 'would be my grandfather's groom, old Carter.' The man had worked on that farm fifty years earlier, and had died in the very stable into which Hazel saw him disappear. What was the scene she saw? A reproduction of the old groom's last few minutes on earth when he might well have felt ill or afraid and generated enough feeling for this to be picked up later in time – so much part of his regular routine that the mark of it had bitten deep into the surroundings – as the chariot-wheel marks in Pompeii bit into the stone of the streets? The latter is material, actual, and is to be perceived by the physical eye, the former – who knows what mental perceptive process is at work to translate the picture into the eye of the mind?

Some four years ago I rented a small semi-detached cottage in the village of Little Cawthorpe, which is about three miles from Louth town. It is one of the pleasantest villages in this part of Lincolnshire, with a noisy brook running through its centre and at one point crossing the lane which serves as village street. Once across the ford and you drive past the Royal Oak Inn (known familiarly to locals as 'The Splash') past a series of attractive cottages and houses, past the village duck pond to a crossroads. Here you turn either left for Muckton or right to Haugham and Louth. If you turn right you must pass the old vicarage, which, no longer inhabited by clergy, possesses a ghost of its own. The ghost is that of a dog, which may be heard pattering about the rooms from time to time. I say 'may be', though I have evidence that it has been heard within the last few years. However, the story came to me from Mr John Bourne, whose Louth spectre I mentioned earlier in this chapter.

Mr Bourne's family once owned the Cawthorpe Vicarage and when he and his family first bought the house they came on one or two occasions to deal with the usual problems of scrubbing and cleaning before the furniture could be moved in. On one such occasion, they had finished the work they had come to do, and were about to lock the back door before departing when Mr Bourne's wife thought she heard an animal pattering about in the upstairs rooms. It seemed to her that a dog must have entered the house unseen and have accidentally been shut in. A search was carried out at once, but nothing was found. There was no sign of an animal in the entire building.

This was the first of several such occurrences. Mr Bourne himself suggested that the phantom may be connected with a ghostly white dog – an animal of unusual size – which is said to haunt the neighbourhood of Haugham and Cawthorpe. This in turn may relate to another spectre of the area, a large cow which apparently jumps the surrounding hedges and ditches on its way down from the heights of Haugham Reedings to the village of Cawthorpe in the valley.

I suspect that we have here again a variation of 'Old Shuck', the padfoot, this time as a white rather than a black apparition. It is significant that once again the animal's unusual size is stressed.

My home was on the opposite side of the village from the ford and the inn, and abutted the main road to Louth. The lane and main road link and form a pleasant circular walk for the villagers. On Sunday mornings the dwellers on the stream side of the village frequently amble on their circular tour, and in doing so pass my former home. If one happened to be in the garden on a Sunday morning, a series of greetings and conversations would take place over the garden gate, and one of my most welcome encounters was with an elderly gentleman who had lived in the neighbourhood since childhood.

Mr Harry Borrill is, by anybody's standards, a remarkable man. He is eighty if he is a day, but nimble-minded, well read and with a long, long memory. He was, when I knew him, interested in all forms of history, in mythology, natural history, and ancient lore. He knew a great deal about Cawthorpe and its environs, and even had one or two tales to tell me about witchcraft in the area in former days. However, he was just as enlightening on the subject of hauntings, and two stories in particular were highly detailed and vivid. The third was an experience which had occurred within his own family, and I will begin with this.

Mr Borrill's daughter was at that time living at home, though later she moved into Louth in order to be nearer the hospital where she was nursing. By coincidence, she took over the town flat in which I was then living, and into which I had moved after leaving Cawthorpe. At the time of the story, however, she still lived with her parents.

Cawthorpe lies south-east of Louth, and is approached on the Louth side by a long straight road which passes at one point a plantation; on the west side of the plantation another country lane runs downhill from the Louth–Skegness road to join at right angles the Louth–Mablethorpe route. The right hand side of the lane as you descend is solid woodland, well fenced off from the roadway.

On the day in question Enid Borrill was walking home from the direction of the Louth–Skegness road and approaching Cawthorpe down the hill lane I have just described. It was daylight and a bright day, and she had the plantation in full view on her right as she walked. Then she perceived someone walking ahead of her. She was surprised that it should be a nun, for the nearest convent is at Grimsby, some twenty miles away. She was still more surprised a few minutes later, when the nun turned off the road and walked into the plantation. Enid did not need to inspect the spot to know that there was no gateway into the plantation at that point. The nun had walked straight through a boundary fence!

Miss Borrill was understandably upset, and so were her parents when she described the occurrence to them. Her father, when he related the story to me, was at a loss to explain it.

'It isn't,' he said, 'as though there were a nunnery near by. The nearest is at Grimsby, and the next nearest at Lincoln. She *couldn't* have seen a nun in this area – and walking into the plantation at that.'

I asked him if there had ever been a convent in the Cawthorpe area, but as far as he was aware there hadn't.

For once, however, Harry Borrill had been misinformed. I learned later from John Bourne that certainly a convent had existed at Cawthorpe. It had flourished during the Middle Ages and until Henry VIII's dissolution order. After that the nuns, like hundreds of others throughout England, had been turned adrift into the world to survive as best they might. Many of them must have longed intensely for the security of their erstwhile homes, the nunneries. Perhaps it was a longing of this nature which recalled Enid's ghostly nun to her well-worn path through the Cawthorpe plantation.

The other side of that plantation has a different story to tell, and a ghost – or ghosts – of its own.

I have known that stretch of road from the Louth–Legbourne corner to the commencement of Cawthorpe village proper since I was a child. Halfway down the plantation side lies a gateway, with a rutted cart track leading into it, and a clearing with a decrepit shed lying beyond. All round stand the sentinel trees, conifers mainly, with a sprinkling of deciduous wood.

At no matter what time of year one passes that gateway, there is always a scarf of mist stretching out from it, lying inert across the roadway, like a barrier. On days of brilliant sunshine, on mornings of sparkling frost, that mist-barrier is there, always at the same point, lying still and unwavering across the path.

My father, when a young man and long before he met my mother, was engaged to the miller's daughter at Legbourne Mill. He was in the habit when his day's work was over, of cycling out to Legbourne via Cawthorpe, taking the route by the plantation and then through Watery Lane to the Mill.

He possessed a reasonably modern bicycle as cycling was one of his hobbies, but in those days modernity did not extend to battery-powered lamps. Both front and rear lights were acetylene-powered and the lamps had to be lit by hand.

On one particular night, dark, with a moon about to rise but not yet risen, my father rode on his usual journey to the Mill. He had turned into the plantation stretch which leads to Cawthorpe, and was passing the gateway when the front lamp of his bicycle went out. He dismounted and re-lit the lamp, climbed back on the bicycle and was about to move, when the rear lamp of the cycle went out. He got off the machine again, re-lit the rear lamp and once more prepared to ride off. At that point both front and rear lamps were extinguished together.

The young man was now thoroughly alarmed and disconcerted. As far as he could see, there was no earthly reason why even one lamp, still less both, should go out. Once more he re-lit both lights, and thereupon jumped on the bike, and pedalled hell-for-leather down the lane. Once out of the mysterious gateway, both lamps remained alight. He came home by the main road through Legbourne village, and for several weeks gave the plantation road a wide berth.

Forty years later when I went to live in Cawthorpe, the plantation road still held its scarf of mist, and not only I, but many of the village's inhabitants, felt a sense of unease when passing the place.

I asked Harry Borrill to tell me of its history and he raised his bushy eyebrows in surprise that I should not know the story. It came in two parts and he told me the latter half first.

On a Christmas morning several years ago, a local man was walking from Cawthorpe to the pub, in Legbourne village, intent on a friendly drink with his cronies to celebrate the season. As he drew level with the plantation gateway, he heard the sound of footsteps approaching behind him. Feeling sociable, he slowed down to enable the man to catch him up, thinking to have a pleasant chat along the road to the inn. The steps came nearer, drew level and then passed him, but *there was no person to be seen*. Immediately following this unpleasant discovery, a herd of pigs dashed past him and he was forced to leap aside to avoid them. When he regained his balance enough to look around, there were no pigs in sight.

As soon as he reached the pub, he told a friend of his experience. He half-expected to be greeted by laughter or disbelief, but surprisingly his friend nodded.

'Aye,' he said, 'when I was ditching there a few years ago, a lady in a car stopped and asked me about yon place. Said there was a stone near by to commemorate a murder. It seems that some time in the 1800s, a drover had taken his stock to Louth market and came back with a herd of pigs he'd bought and a pocket full of money from the sale of his own stock. Somebody was lying in wait for him in that gateway, jumped out on him and cut his throat. The stone the lady spoke about had been taken away by the soldiers in the last war. Don't know what became of it.'

It seems the scarf of mist has replaced the stone as a *memento mori* in that particular place.

Mr Borrill had an even eerier tale to tell of the village to the south of Legbourne. Muckton is less a village than a hamlet, and its bucolic name belies its attractive setting. The few houses are piled together round a sharp bend of road, with slight rises in the ground to give shape and interest to church and vicarage. There is a scattering of trees, with, on the horizon, the remains of Muckton Wood with its large and famous heronry.

Between the wars a young couple moved into a cottage in the village and settled down to their reasonably-new married life. It was a tied cottage and the man worked on the land for the farmer-owner, as was (and in some parts of the country, still is) the custom in an agricultural community.

The cottage was pleasant and dry in spite of the fact that it had been unoccupied for a considerable time before the young people moved into it. The fact that it was cold could be accounted for by the brick floors which were placed over the solid earth.

They moved in at midwinter, and at first nothing unusual was noticed. One night, however, an inexplicable occurrence took place.

The man came home after a day's work, tired and ready for a meal. He took off his muddy boots and placed them together under the kitchen table. No sooner had he done so than he thought the boots moved. Hardly believing the evidence of his eyes, he looked again and without doubt the boots were moving slowly and deliberately under the table. As soon as they were removed and placed in a corner, they remained perfectly motionless.

The pattern of this occurrence was repeated several days running and both husband and wife observed the phenomenon. Whenever the boots were placed beneath the table they moved. At first the movements were gentle, but after a time they grew more agitated and determined. In time the table itself began gently to rock. Finally it seemed to the couple that the movement of the boots appeared to simulate walking. They could no longer stand living in the house.

A clergyman was consulted, and on his advice the floor of the kitchen was taken up. There in the middle of the room, beneath the area where the table had stood, was found the skeleton of a man, uncoffined and unidentifiable.

The remains were removed and given consecrated burial. The cottage stood empty for a time but was re-occupied at a later date. There is no evidence of any subsequent disturbance having taken place and eventually the building was demolished.

No information has ever come to light regarding the identity of the buried corpse, and the whole story remains as mysterious now as it was at the time of the young couple's disturbed tenancy. *How* such a physical manifestation could occur is beyond my ingenuity to explain. One is tempted to say 'hallucination' and leave it at that. But both man and wife saw the boots move, and on several occasions. And if it were hallucination, then the presence of an apparently hastily buried corpse on the site is too extreme a coincidence to be acceptable as such. One is forced to the conclusion that there must be some connection between corpse and manifestation. This is one of the few supernatural occurrences I have encountered which refuses to fit into a pattern.

The same cannot be said of two stories relating to another area of north

Lincolnshire, however. The Irby 'boggle' – 'boggle' being a variant of the term 'bogy' – is that of a girl, Rosamund Guy, betrothed to a man named Neville Randall. On the evening of 1 November 1455, and just before they were due to be married, the couple met in Irby Dale woods. A violent quarrel occurred during which Randall killed his fiancée. The girl's father swore that her ghost would haunt the place until the man was brought to justice. It appears that some presence is still felt in the neighbourhood. My informant for this story, Mr R. A. Robinson, of Cherry Willingham, near Lincoln, assures me that horses have shied at the spot when forced to pass it. One suspects that any remnants of the girl's presence are a result of her own acute terror rather than a prediction or curse of her father's. It is illogical and unlikely that a living human being can superimpose his will upon a dead.

I am indebted to Mr Robinson for the story of another haunting, that of a milkmaid named Molly Briars, who was killed on a hillside near the village of Beelsby. The stone she used as a stool is still to be found on the hillside where Molly milked her cows, and her ghost troubles the vicinity. Local legend has it that ill-luck will come upon the village of Beelsby if the stone is ever moved, and to this day no local person is disposed to touch it.

The 'legend' part of this tale has obviously arisen from the 'ghost' part of it. Haunted sites can hardly be regarded as lucky, and in unsophisticated communities taboos and superstitions find an easy focus on such areas.

There are two stories of Lincolnshire hauntings, which, though they depart from the general tone of this book in that they were not experienced in this century, are nevertheless of great historical interest.

The first concerns Epworth Rectory, the childhood home of John Wesley. The story is well enough known, though I have not heard of any contemporary manifestations.

During the incumbency of Wesley's father the Rectory was said to be haunted by a poltergeist, although its behaviour does not seem to have been typical of that kind of occurrence. Various noises were heard about the house; footsteps up and down stairs, mumblings, the sound of breaking bottles, the sound of dancing, the noise of a turkey-cock gobbling, the sound of a nightgown swishing along the ground. Mr Wesley himself on one occasion (inevitably, at night. Why are ghosts so nocturnal in their habits?) heard nine distinct knocks in the room next door to his own. The knocks were divided into sets of three, with a pause at the end of every third. The rector went into the next room but found it empty, and thinking it might be some ill-wishing parishioner playing tricks – the Wesleys had their enemies in the parish – he took his mastiff dog along to investigate. The dog was terrified and ran back to his master for protection. On another occasion Robin Brown, the manservant, took the dog into his room for company and to guard against the night's disturbances. However, when the latch began to move and rattle as usual, the dog crept into bed and howled its terror to the entire house.

No one knows to this day how far the 'poltergeist' was a genuine haunting and how far it was the work of hostile elements within the Epworth parish. Certainly the recorded manifestations seem to follow the common forms, though of the individual 'pattern' type haunting rather than the poltergeist type.

The second story is of the 'one-off' type, in that it occurred on a single occasion only. But it has a charm associated with the tale's principals, and with the particular setting in which the incident took place.

The village of Somersby lies between Louth and Horncastle, in a fold of the

Lincolnshire Wolds. It is secluded, shaded, dreaming, the perfect birthplace for a great poet; for however Tennyson's reputation has slipped since his death, there is no denying the stature of 'Ulysses' or much of 'In Memoriam'.

The Tennysons, also, were an ecclesiastical family. Alfred's father, George Tennyson, was Rector of Somersby and Bag Enderby, and the old Somersby Rectory lies directly opposite the village church.

It is an attractive house, long and low, with a garden shut away from the country lane which separates it from the church.

The house is in private occupation and is not open to the public. However, I have been lucky enough to see it and was shown over the building some years ago by the wife of the present owner. Lady Maitland pointed out to me the attic where Alfred's early writing was done, the mock-Gothic dining-hall which the rector and his sons built between them, and the lawned gardens at the back of the house where the Tennyson girls used to sit on summer evenings.

Alfred's sister, Emily, was engaged to Arthur Hallam, close friend and companion of the poet. Hallam was a frequent visitor to Somersby and was much loved by all the family. It was customary for family and guests to gather on the lawns on soft summer nights, sometimes to make music and sing, sometimes to talk or wander down to the brook at the garden's foot. Tennyson described garden, stream, house and village often enough in his work for it to be plain how greatly the setting influenced him.

It is not difficult to imagine the scene – the girls pretty in their summer crinolines, the young men full of laughter and talk; the whole scene closed in by the house, the brook, and the tall trees where the rooks and doves talked the warm evenings away.

*Somersby Rectory. From the Tennyson Research Centre, Lincoln. By kind permission of Lincolnshire Library Service*

The year was 1833, the time September. Arthur Hallam had gone to Tyrol and Vienna on holiday with his father. He wrote both to Emily and Alfred and his last letter was dated 6 September. A week later, he was dead. His father returned from a walk to find Arthur apparently asleep on the couch, but he had suffered a cerebral thrombosis.

At Somersby one evening just before this event, Matilda and Mary Tennyson had taken a stroll down the lane outside the house. They had gone only a short distance when they saw a tall figure clothed in white walking ahead of them. Presently it turned aside and walked through the hedge, where both girls knew there was no gap or gateway. Tilly was so disturbed by the occurrence that on reaching home she burst into tears. A few days later she attended a dancing lesson at Spilsby, and collected there the letters for Somersby, one of which was addressed to her brother, Alfred.

The poet read the letter at the dinner-table, but immediately left the table, and shortly afterwards asked Emily to come to him. He told her then the terrible news.

The Tennysons later concluded that the appearance of the white figure had occurred at approximately the time of Arthur's death. In any case, this seems to be an instance similar to that in my own family, where the figure appears as a herald or warning of imminent death. Impossible to guess how such a manifestation can take place.

One last story from Lincolnshire again from my friend, Hazel Willows.

A certain old house in Weelsby Road, Grimsby, is built on the site of a former nunnery. From time to time the occupants have heard the noise of footsteps walking about the premises, and occasional sounds of heavy and laboured breathing. It is known that the Mother Superior of the convent was a chronic asthmatic; it is therefore logical to suppose that the sounds are echoes of her former occupation of the premises.

There are ghosts in other parts of this large county – one at Thornton Abbey, one at Sleaford, another at Boston – and I daresay these are but a fraction of the total number of hauntings in Lincolnshire.

# SUFFOLK
## Smugglers, Two Children and the Handsome Earl of Sandwich

Suffolk is one of my favourite counties. There is a softness in its air and landscape which marks if off from the lands farther north. It has the great wide skies of Norfolk, plus a remarkably varied topography and a comparatively gentle climate. It is a county of sharp contrasts. Narrow, banked lanes, wild-flower fringed; acres of open heathland; wooded areas whose picnic places alternate with mysteriously thick forests; a beautiful coastline of cliffs and little fishing towns. It is not surprising that the county is favoured by writers and artists, many of whom have settled in its picturesque villages.

The little towns and villages are worth travelling miles to visit. The names ring strangely on the tongue: Saxmundham, Long Melford, Walberswick, Lavenham, Blythburgh, Framlingham. Many of them are associated with the wool and weaving days, and the architecture echoes the high times of merchant wealth and prosperity.

Inevitably, the old associations cling. Stories are handed down until they become part of local tradition. In mid-county the traditions are mainly concerned with agriculture and the cottage weaving industry; on the coast they are bolder, as befits a fishing, sea-going people. The stories there are of smuggling and battles with the king's Customs. Both areas have their tales of haunting and the spectres are as varied as the county itself.

One story for which I have as yet found neither parallel nor explanation is that of the dancing ghosts of Saxmundham. My informant is Mr B. Waterman, of Ipswich, who, during his boyhood, lived at Saxmundham. He and his brother were quite young children at the time of the occurrence, the first being nine years old, the other two years younger.

The children left their home one morning intending to play in Carlton Park, about half a mile away. Their route lay along Harper's Lane and involved passing a row of stables and a stretch of open meadowland.

The boys had walked past the stables when, to use Mr Waterman's phrase, they 'pulled up dead in their tracks'. In a meadow about thirty yards away, they saw seven or eight figures dancing in a circle. Each was dressed in a white, luminous muslin garment which covered the wearer from head to foot. The dancers moved with natural movements of the limbs and now, remembering the occasion many years afterwards, Mr Waterman describes the dance as being similar to ballet. 'A kind of follow-my-leader, in a circle'. There was no music accompanying the scene, neither were the dancers' faces visible. After several seconds the figures disappeared. The children looked at each other, then ran back down the lane. Strangely, they did not mention the incident to their parents, but this may have been because shortly afterwards they encountered friends from the town, and in the resulting play, what they had seen near Harper's Lane dwindled in importance.

Mr Waterman knows of no story associated with the area. The only building in this desolate spot at that time was an ancient inn, the Bottle and Glass, which stood by the old Rendham–Saxmundham road. The pub has since been pulled down, and although some time after the ghost incident the Waterman family lived in this old hostelry, they never again saw the dancing figures.

At the time of the manifestation, neither child knew what a ghost was, and it appears not to have occurred to the boys that anything untoward had happened. As men, however, both clearly recollect the incident and are agreed about its details.

The experience of Mr P. M. Warwick was more usual – more usual, that is, in the terms of the patterns of psychic manifestation!

Mr Warwick volunteered to help a friend convert a cellar into a workshop. The cellar lay below shop premises in Haverhill, and neither man had any reason to think the place haunted. The work had hardly begun, however, when noises were heard in the shop overhead. The men stopped work in order to investigate the sounds, but the noises immediately ceased.

A similar situation arose the next night, and on several other occasions when the shop was closed.

The two friends were sufficiently intrigued to wish to investigate further, and it seemed to them that an independent witness would be desirable. They therefore invited a third acquaintance to join them one evening, forbearing to mention their own experiences.

During the evening, the third man was asked to go into a back room to fill a kettle with water. This room was situated at the foot of the flight of stairs leading to the shop premises.

Almost immediately the pair in the workshop heard footsteps ascending the stairs. The friend, as it happened, was still busy with the kettle and never approached the stairs at any time.

The same test was tried with two other individuals, neither of whom was aware of the situation. In each case the result was the same.

Eventually the tenant of the workshop was forced to relinquish the room because of the nervous strain which the manifestations imposed on him.

The degree of nervous strain caused to 'receivers' of psychic manifestations seem to vary. In some cases severe shock seems to be suffered; in others, depression and fear; in still others there is tolerance and curiosity. The greatest degree of shock seems to be experienced by those who had, until the moment of their experience, been totally sceptical regarding psychic phenomena.

One such was a lorry driver travelling the East Anglian area. The man, whose home is in Grimsby, was driving along the A12 road from Ipswich, making for Kessingland, where he usually stayed when in the district. He had reached the area which traverses Blythburgh Common, and the road, at this point, runs up and down a series of small hills.

It was a bright, clear night and he could see some distance ahead. The road was perfectly empty and as he topped one rise he could see across to the next. There was no traffic in sight. However, as he swung up the next hill, to his consternation he saw less than twenty yards ahead of him two people leading a large black horse. His mind registered the man as wearing breeches, boots and a skirted coat ('dressed like a highwayman', to use the driver's own words). The female figure was that of a girl between twenty and twenty-five, wearing a long dress, frilled at the hem. She appeared to be holding her hat clutched against her skirt.

The lorry was on top of the figures before the driver's brakes could bite. Convinced that he had hit and probably killed at least one of the figures in the road, the man pulled the truck to a screeching halt, clambered out and ran round to the front of the cab. The roadway was empty, the entire scene blank of any living presence save his own. He had been keyed for one moment of horror; he experienced another.

A much-shaken man drove his lorry into Kessingland that evening. He told his landlady, Mrs Elaine Burke, that he had never believed in ghosts until that moment, but was now convinced that what he had seen was supernatural.

The driver is a steady, reliable man and far from given to flights of fancy.

As this particular manifestation occurred only six weeks before the original draft of this chapter was written it seemed necessary to turn over as many stones as possible in order to uncover the history of the haunting. I therefore enquired extensively in the Blythburgh area and emerged with some interesting facts.

The ghostly horse, man and girl have been seen on several occasions during the last two hundred years, and while there is some divergence of opinion regarding the identity of the man, certain facts are agreed upon. The man – either a farmer or farm labourer – worked land in the neighbourhood of the Common. His niece, of whom he was very fond, was accustomed to bring his lunch at midday on whatever part of the farm he chanced to be working. Legend has it – and I suspect this to be a 'word-of-mouth' handed down story, whose factual details are likely to have changed little with time – that he dropped dead while ploughing and the girl found him lying beside his horse.

It is a likely enough story, and the intensity of the girl's emotions at the time could well have fixed the pattern on the physical surroundings.

One interesting feature emerges: occasionally the girl is seen riding the horse rather than holding her uncle's arm. The reason for this variation at present escapes me. However, the picture-image is usually of three figures – horse, man and girl. The dress places it inescapably in the eighteenth century.

Two weeks after I wrote the story of this haunting and its attendant local legends, the lorry driver himself telephoned me. He held certain positive views which should be put on record, since they conflict with aspects of the local history.

He placed the age of the girl as in her early twenties (some local reports speak of her as a child); the age of the man as being about twenty-six to twenty-eight. This makes the uncle-niece relationship an unlikely though not impossible one.

The driver was also convinced that the man's dress was not that of a peasant, but of a gentleman. His second description to me suggested conventional male riding-dress of the period, more appropriate to a man of property than to a ploughman. Beyond this it is not possible to go at the present time.

Blythburgh Common is noted for another ghostly presence; that of Black Toby, a Negro soldier said to be a drummer with troops stationed near by in the year 1754. According to local tradition, the man was convicted of murdering a servant girl on the common, and sentenced to be hanged. He pleaded to be allowed to be dragged at the end of a rope by the mailcoach, but the local judiciary would have none of this gentle treatment and insisted on the hanging. The man was duly executed on a nearby gibbet and since that time his spirit has been seen at intervals in the neighbourhood. Occasionally, I am told, the spectre is that of a coach drawn by headless horses – presumably the mailcoach which the drummer had requested as the method of execution!

The story of a single spectre – that of Toby himself – seems credible, for part of the Common is still known as 'Toby's Walks', and the name may have grown from local experiences. In the headless horses I frankly do not believe.

*The White Hart, Blythburgh*

This inexplicable decapitation smacks too much of imaginative embroidery. If there is a coach and horse phantom – and East Anglia has many – I think it is unconnected with the Toby legend.

Although I made extensive enquiries in the neighbourhood, I could not find any record of the Toby manifestation within recent times. I have no doubt that a barn in the vicinity known as Toby's Barn, is, like the 'Walks', an authentic association with the original story.

The village of Blythburgh has ghosts of its own. Blythburgh Priory is said to be the setting for one haunting. Stealthy footsteps have been heard on back and front stairs of the old house, and in a passageway. Certain parts of garden and grounds are avoided by animals. This is hearsay only. I met no one who had recent evidence.

There is evidence, however, of a haunting of The White Hart at Blythburgh, which is situated on the opposite side of the main road to Ipswich.

This is a venerable and attractive pub, famous for its good food and the friendliness of its licensees.

To say that the place is old conveys little idea of its mellowness or its beauty. The building was at one time the ancient Ecclesiastical Court House and was associated with the nearby priory. The 'modern' part of the building is fifteenth century, the older section thirteenth century.

From outside appearances it is impossible to judge the pub's age. It is a black and white construction, strongly proportioned, and set against the grey-green backdrop of a sea-marsh, which at full-tide turns into a glittering mere.

Within the building, the fine carved beams catch the eye, and the great inglenook fireplaces at either end of the bar.

Behind the long bar counter is a solid oak door leading to the living quarters of the house. It is on this door that a knocking has been heard. 'As though,' the licensee's wife said, 'the person who knocked wore a ring.' The building was, you will remember, the Ecclesiastical Court House. The prior, head of the nearby religious settlement, would almost certainly wear a ring as part of his official insignia. It is equally sure that his duties must have caused him to visit the Court House from time to time.

Footsteps have been heard in the house, also, but for a considerable time now there have been no manifestations at The White Hart. The reason may be once again that the material surroundings have been disturbed. A fire took place two or three years ago at one end of the room which is now used as a bar. Considerable damage was done and repair work was necessary. Since that time neither footsteps nor knockings have been heard.

Another tale associated with the pub suggests that at one time the place may have been used for witchcraft, though personally I think smuggling is a more likely explanation.

The story is that 'a little man with a black stick' used to raise the devil in the pub, and that the said devil, which was only a foot high, materialised vertically through the concrete. An interesting bit of fantasy, this. You will notice how none of this story hangs together. Why a 'little' man? What was the purpose of the black stick? Was it a wand? Why such a small devil? Was this relative to the size of the necromancer? And what is the likelihood of concrete's being in use at the period when this hocus-pocus is said to have taken place?

There may be a shadow of truth in the tale somewhere. Witchcraft *may* have been conducted on the premises. However, I am more inclined to think the story would be put about by the neighbourhood's smuggling fraternity as a deterrent to unwelcome strangers.

Moving along from Blythburgh to Walberswick, one encounters rumours of hauntings in Dead Man's Gulley. Apparently this is the site of an old railway line, and I was told by a local horsewoman that horses always shy at this place, seemingly upset by something invisible to their riders. The local name for the area is significant. A railway line does not become known as Dead Man's Gulley for no reason. Whose was the corpse? And is it his presence which the horses sense? Unanswerable questions until more information comes to light on the subject.

It is strange that some stories are preserved in great detail and handed down by word-of-mouth tradition over several centuries, while others, possibly no less old, quickly became blurred and forgotten, until only a faint echo of the original tale survives. Is this traditional remembering a question of interest or preference? Does the race select what it will remember and preserve? And if so, on what basis is the selection made?

I found myself asking these questions when I visited Walberswick, which is one of the most delightful villages in Suffolk.

I had expected the village to have at least as many stories as neighbouring Blythburgh, but very little came to light upon enquiry.

Once or twice Blythwood or Westwood Lodge was mentioned as being reputedly haunted by a phantom in a silk dress. A local inhabitant referred to the ghost as 'the white woman', but knew no details of the haunting. I heard a rumour that a policeman had spent the night there within recent memory, and had a nasty experience, but since everyone I talked to on the subject was deliciously vague, I am little wiser now concerning the white woman than I was when I entered the village.

Mr Winyard of Walberswick was, however, informative on the subject of a ghost at the old Anchor Inn in the village.

The new Anchor Inn was built in the 1920s and moved some fifty yards back from the site of the original pub, which was pulled down at that time. The new Anchor is ghost-free, I understand, but the old pub was part of the smuggling scene, and when the building was pulled down a bricked-up doorway was found in the cellar. Later, when the water supply to the new building was being laid on, workmen discovered an underground passageway. These are certainly smugglers' trappings, but the origin of the ghost story is less obvious.

Mr Winyard and his brother shared a bedroom when they were boys, and although 'Ginger' Winyard himself never heard anything untoward in the old Anchor, his brother several times heard the sound of an old mangle being turned. This invariably occurred at midnight, and was frequently accompanied by all the bedclothes falling off the bed. A strange sequence, indeed. Unlikely that any woman would have been in the *habit* of washing and mangling at midnight – unless she had muddy, or bloody, clothes to clean before they were seen by inquisitive neighbours.

Guesswork of this kind does not explain the odd behaviour of the bedclothes, of course.

As it happens, bedclothes are frequently involved in ghostly manifestations. They are pulled back, thrown to the floor, crumpled or just plain sat upon. One does not hear of activities of this nature in connection with tablecloths, curtains or tea-towels – just bedclothes. I found a similar incident to the above in a Southwold ghost story.

Southwold is just across the haven from Walberswick, and a ferry operates between the two in good weather. If you wish to make the journey by road, the distance is far longer, though the drive is worth the trouble, since it goes by breckland and sea-marsh and along a winding country lane or two.

In spite of a regular influx of tourists during the summer season, Southwold has preserved intact its old-world character, and has an air of being in the twentieth century but not of it.

Much of the town's atmosphere comes from the several fine old buildings which are still to be found among the modern and modernised shop fronts. It is surprising that so much of value remains since the old town was largely destroyed by a disastrous fire in the year 1659.

One house which survived the fire would be worth visiting solely on account of its architectural value. Sutherland House, facing on to the main street, once was known as 'Cammels', and was so called after the wealthy Elizabethan merchant who owned it. The house was apparently built as early as 1455, though the beautiful moulded ceilings were not constructed until the time of the Armada. They exist today, looking much the same as they must have done then – darker, yellower, with small chips and cracks to be seen here and there, but intact, impressive and still a joy to the eye. They attract many sightseers, but the house is no longer a stranger to visitors, for the downstairs premises are now used as tea-rooms, and there is a continual coming and going of people who visit as much for the history of the surroundings as for the home-made produce served there.

But Sutherland House has claims to fame other than sheer age. During

*Sutherland House, Southwold*

Charles II's reign, war with the Dutch resulted in a sea battle being fought off the Suffolk coast. The battle of Sole ( a contraction of S'wold) Bay brought to the town certain dignitaries, including, so tradition has it, James, Duke of York, himself, and Edward Montague, Earl of Sandwich, Commander aboard the flagship *Royal James*.

Now battle commanders must sleep somewhere on the eve of battle, and in those days this did not necessarily mean with the army or navy commanded. The Earl of Sandwich chose to sleep at the house known as Cammels, as did the Royal Duke. The building became a temporary military HQ.

Tradition also has it that a young maidservant was employed in the house, a red-haired girl of sixteen, who slept in an attic on the top floor.

After the arrival of the commanders, however, apparently the young redhead attracted some attention and as a result changed her sleeping quarters to the large and beautiful room on the first floor which was occupied by Lord Sandwich.

Now it's all hearsay, of course. How can anyone be *sure* what happened on the night before the morning of a battle three hundred years ago? It is said that on 28 May 1672, the Earl overslept and was late aboard his flagship. So late that the battle was already in progress when he arrived. So late that local rumour persists in asserting that his tardiness cost the English the battle. The battle of Sole Bay was actually neither lost nor won; it was one of those indecisive engagements with which naval history is littered. Both sides claimed a victory, neither admitted defeat. Sandwich himself was killed in action and the little redhead waited in vain for his return.

But did she? Let us look at the evidence.

The first I heard of this particular haunting, was a story that a young girl had been seen looking from the window of a first-floor room of Sutherland House. The girl was said to be red haired. During my stay in Southwold, I did not meet anyone who had experienced this aspect of the apparition, but the present owner of the old house, Mrs Patricia Jones, had more detailed and more interesting information to impart.

Mrs Jones, her husband and her aunt have all experienced manifestations of some kind in the house. Mrs Jones's aunt actually sleeps in the room said to be haunted – the main bedroom on the first floor.

Each of the occupants has heard footsteps in the corridors connecting the rooms, sounds of someone walking downstairs and the noise of doors opening and closing. These events apparently take place only occasionally, although there is one particular night of the year when they have always been present during the Joneses' ownership of the building – that is, on the eve of the anniversary of the battle of Sole Bay, 28 May.

There was one occasion which Mrs Jones remembers particularly clearly. A young student was staying in the house at the time, and occupied one of the attic bedrooms on the second floor.

The Joneses woke about 2.00 a.m. to hear footsteps descending the stairs from the attic. No light was switched on, which they thought strange, but they assumed that the girl student was going downstairs to get a drink of water and perhaps had enough light from her bedroom to illumine the stairhead and well. The steps sounded along the landing then began to descend the second flight. The listener heard every stair creak as it was trodden on. At the foot of the stairs is an old door with a drop latch. They heard the latch lift and the door open. They lay and waited for their young guest to return. But the door did not close, nor did they hear any footsteps returning to the attic bedroom.

When Mrs Jones came down the next morning, the oak door was firmly shut, and the student, when asked, said she had never been out of bed the previous night.

The household possesses a cat, a venerable Siamese named Twinkle. The animal is a much-loved pet and has the complete run of the house, wandering in and out of rooms at will. The one room she will not enter is the front room occupied by Mrs Jones's aunt.

There was one occasion when the cat accidentally became shut in this bedroom, and when let out, showed signs of extreme fear, spitting and shooting downstairs at great speed. Being old, the animal is usually slow-moving.

There was another time when the room's occupant was away for a few days and the bedroom was kept shut up. No one entered the room and it had been left in apple-pie order. Yet when Mr Jones himself went in before Aunt Emma returned, he found that furniture had been moved, and that the bedspread was crumpled, as though someone had been lying on it.

On the latest anniversary of the battle of Sole Bay, the Joneses were awakened, as usual, in the early hours. They were happy to assume that the cat was responsible for the sound which awakened them – until they saw that the animal was sound asleep on their bed.

Mr Jones himself felt 'a cold shiver' and as though he had 'walked through cobwebs'. Both these are descriptions we have met elsewhere in connection with hauntings, and shall doubtless meet again.

I was anxious to see the interior of the house, not only because of its relevance to my research, but for its own sake – for a certain beautiful and remote quality which seems to cling to some historic buildings.

The two main ground floor rooms, as I have said, are open to the public. Their interest lies in their ceilings and in two portraits which hang either side of the great brick fireplace of one room. But leaving these, we walked up the narrow wooden stair – creaking at every step – along the corridor to the front bedroom.

I found it a well-proportioned room, lighted by two windows, one of which looks out upon the street. Once more, as in the Oxfam shop in Norwich's Magdalen Street, there was the indefinable sense of 'presence'; a concentration of energy, or a displacement of air, I do not know which. Whichever it was, the area of the concentration was between front window and bed and in terms of distance about six feet from the window.

Unlike the Magdalen Street presence, the feeling here was of happiness, almost, I was about to write, of childish happiness. The sensation was at once joyful and gentle.

When we visited the attic bedroom which traditionally was that of the young maid, feeling was almost totally absent. It was as though the grand front room was the place where the girl had been happiest in life. And perhaps death had offered her nothing better.

Whatever emotion was generated here the night before the naval battle appears to have remained.

I looked at the portrait of Lord Sandwich on my way out. A round, pleasant face, sensual and amiable. What was the name of the peasant child who fell in love with it?

Southwold is rich in ghosts. At the far end of the street from Sutherland House stands another building of considerable age – Denny's, the outfitters, an establishment of sufficient quality to be known over a considerable area of Suffolk.

Mr Denny is a cultivated man whose family have resided in the town for longer than anyone living there can remember. In fact for many years Sutherland House itself was owned by one branch of his family.

Mr Denny is a strict non-believer in ghosts. However, he has twice heard the sound of footsteps walking across the floor of the room over his shop. Has twice investigated, and on each occasion found the room unoccupied.

It was Mr Denny's daughter, Mrs Lyn Knight, who told me of having ridden a horse through Dead Man's Gulley, only to have the animal shy violently at a certain spot. Other accounts confirmed this type of animal behaviour at that place.

There are many stories of hauntings in Southwold. Some have survived with a wealth of detail, bolstered from time to time by local encounters with a particular phantom. Other tales are more faded, less authenticated. Such are the phantom Lady of Shuck's Hill, who is said to appear with her dog; and the woman in black who occasionally materialises from the cliff face and was seen by two fishermen named Swann and Ellis eight or nine years ago. That the apparition comes out of the solid cliff suggests that her place of exit may once have been a cave-mouth, long since blocked up. Perhaps another smuggling link. Another little-seen spectre is that of a fisherman carrying a Tilley lamp and with a large fish slung over one shoulder as he walks along the beach.

A more thoroughly documented haunting is that of the soldier on Gun Hill, Southwold, who is said to stand beside one of the old cannon which point out to sea from the cliff-top. The story runs that the young gunner had his head blown off when one of the cannon exploded. Inevitably the variations in the ghost story include the presence of a *headless* gunner. I was even told by one *raconteur* that the soldier was fired from the gun! Usually, however, one finds that the simple bones of the story represent the facts; the frills came later, added by those with a taste for imaginative reconstruction – or leg-pulling.

There are two further stories before we leave Southwold. One was told me by the licensee of The Victoria Inn.

Around the turn of the century the pub's licensee was a Captain Jarvis. His presence is said frequently to have manifested itself in his old environment. Doors have opened of their own accord; objects have fallen off the walls and on one occasion a barrel of beer in the cellar was moved, although no human agency had been near it.

The other tale concerns a house, or rather two houses, on the outskirts of the town. These houses were built identically, and were occupied by two sisters. The tale I heard in Southwold town was that the sisters loved the same man and quarrelled as a result. The story I had from the occupants of one of the houses contained nothing of the romantic aspect of the tale, but did speak directly of certain manifestations which had occurred.

The Boydens have lived in the house over twenty-seven years, and have brought up their family there. Mrs Boyden has heard a man's footsteps walking on the stairs – but walking apparently on bare boards. There have also been sounds of heavy breathing in certain rooms.

The dining-room in particular seems to be a focus for manifestation. The Boydens' elder son has felt a sensation of intense cold in the room, when apparently there was no reason for it. The family cat reacts in the usual animal way, by bristling and exhibiting fear.

Mr Boyden, who affirms non-belief in hauntings, has remarked on hearing the sound of swishing taffeta.

All the family have experienced the switching on and off of lights in the house. There has sometimes been a light sound, as of a cat jumping when their own cat has been placidly sitting with the family.

As for the second house, a woman in a grey dress is said to have been seen in its garden, though the Boydens had no personal knowledge of this.

The house had 'atmosphere' – not strongly marked, nor unpleasant, but just enough to make one sharply aware of one's surroundings. The Boydens themselves seemed singularly pleasant and happy people. They do not ignore the manifestations, but accommodate them, and appear undisturbed by the extra-human activities.

While researching in this area, I stayed with a friend at Wangford, who suggested that the Queen's Head at Blyford possessed historic and ghostly associations.

Although I lived for a short time in the area a few years ago, I had not visited this particular inn. It was therefore a pleasant surprise to find the thatched building lying long and low beside the road which separated it from the parish church.

The church is worth visiting if you collect old churches. Blyford church is Saxon, founded in AD 993, and inside has a certain gaunt aura of impregnability.

*The Church and Queen's Head inn, Blyford*

Perhaps it was this quality, borne out by the thick stone walls and the general isolation of the setting, which prompted the old smugglers to use it as a hiding place. Local tradition avers that barrels of grog found their way under the pews and even under the altar. 'Brandy for the parson, baccy for the clerk . . .'

The inn was conveniently situated a stone's throw away, and the usual ubiquitous underground passageways formed the link. Inside the Queen's Head a relic of one of the passages has been discovered in the cellar – discreetly bricked up.

However, the advent of (comparatively) law-abiding times does not appear to have put an end to the habitual activities of the past. The pub's landlord and his wife have experienced some inexplicable occurrences during their tenancy of the five-hundred-year-old building. I talked to each in turn one busy Sunday morning when the bar was full and conversation had perforce to be conducted in snatches.

The wife's encounters differed significantly from those of her husband, and this was an interesting feature of the manifestations. The lady had seen lights in the building on many occasions – twice they appeared as four bluish lights in the bedroom which, as she described the incident, 'vanished through the wardrobe'. She had also heard some noises, but did not seem able to identify them as having particular characteristics.

Her husband had not seen lights, but he had heard noises on many occasions, and was able accurately to describe them. Apparently they differed in kind; sometimes they were particularly loud and booming, like explosions; on other occasions they were sharp cracks. He heard footsteps occasionally but these had also been heard by his wife. The manifestations seem to occur at any time and are not specifically limited to the hours of darkness.

Then an interesting fact emerged; there had, he said, been one time when a manifestation had taken place when the bar was full, and everyone present had heard the sounds. On this occasion there had been the noise of footsteps walking about in the upstairs room. Both the landlord and his clients decided that someone had broken into the premises from the rear and was rifling the upper floors while the occupants were engaged downstairs.

It happened that among the pub's clients that day were two policemen enjoying an off-duty drink. Hearing the noise of the intruder, they raced up to investigate. They found the upstairs rooms totally deserted, with no sign that anything had been disturbed or anyone had trespassed there. They came down somewhat at a loss and not a little uneasy.

By now conversation in the bar was entirely of the mystery. A couple in one corner, who were spending the summer in the area and often visited the Queen's Head, added to the effect by saying that they had heard these noises on several previous occasions, but had not spoken of it to the licensee for fear of alarming him. By the time the incident was concluded and closing time arrived, not only the landlord was alarmed.

One particularly striking fact emerged. Some time after the present licensees took over the inn, certain structural alterations were made, in the course of which the underground passageway referred to earlier was discovered. It is only since these alterations that the manifestations have occurred. This sounds like further proof of my theory that the material surroundings hold the imprint of emotions and events – or of emotions generated by events.

And what events would give rise to a sequence of incidents like those described?

In an interesting booklet called *Smugglers of the Suffolk Coast*, Leonard P. Thomson tells of battles between smugglers and excise men in this area, and of the old Queen's Head being used as a smuggling headquarters.

Look at the evidence. There is the sound of heavy footsteps. A man does not need to be large in physique to produce a heavy tread; an average man carrying a considerable weight – say a barrel or cask – will also tread heavily. There are bluish lights vanishing through the wardrobe. No doubt candles or tapers were in use, and where the landlord's wardrobe now stands, there may have once been a door. There is a booming sound, which could be that of an explosion; there are noises like cracks – and the sound of pistol shots would produce just such a sound. I believe that what the occupants of the Queen's Head hear are the sounds of a running fight between smugglers and king's men, which may have taken place at some time in the pub's darker history.

> Laces for a lady, letters for a spy,
> And watch the wall, my darling, while the
> gentlemen go by.

The interview I had with these good folk, who were most helpful in spite of being extremely busy at the time, resulted in some interest being taken in our conversation by customers at the bar.

Several of these were regulars, and I suspect that many knew the stories of the area and could have filled out the picture had they wished. However, a strong and discreet silence was maintained and no one was willing to be drawn on the subject of the haunting. East Anglians are good at keeping their mouths shut. They have been accustomed for centuries to not being sure who is who, and which stranger can be trusted. If you've been invaded by everybody from the Romans onwards, you learn when to hold your tongue.

(Watch the wall, my darling, while the
gentlemen go by.)

After I left the Queen's Head I walked over in the bright winter sunshine to view the little church. It stands on a knoll, and has an air of being strong and self-possessed, much like that of a very small castle. The seagulls were gliding past its tower, and a bevy of lapwings performed leisurely aerobatics overhead. The sparkle of the morning set the dark doings of the smugglers at a safe distance. But for the rest of the day the Queen's Head story stayed with me. And that night I thought of the landlord and his lady, sleeping alone in the place, and perhaps listening again for the sounds of conflict.

Away from the coast the smuggling memories fade, to be replaced by hauntings more closely connected with agriculture and the bucolic life. One such homely tale also carries a strong whiff (if you will forgive the unintentional pun, the point of which you will see in the next sentence) of the monastic Middle Ages. It concerns a house thought to have been a resting-place for travelling monks, and the 'ghosts' are the aromas of cooking!

The house is in Lidgate, near Newmarket, and is known as John o' Lydgate's. John, it seems, was a monk of Bury St Edmund's Abbey and a sometime pupil of Chaucer. It is not known how the house came to be associated with him, but he may have been among the mendicant friars who used the place as a hospice.

*Bury St Edmund's Abbey Ruins*

Be that as it may, certain hospitable echoes have remained there. Various occupants have noticed pungent smells of cooking emanating from the old fireplace in a downstairs room. This may have been in use as a refectory for the monks, or as a kitchen.

Two owners in particular have remarked on the manifestations. One, Mrs F. J. Hollingsworth, occupied the house just after the Second World War. One morning, she was seated typing in the downstairs apartment referred to, and concentrating intently on the work before her. She had only recently breakfasted and food was certainly not in her thoughts. Then she noticed a delicious smell of baking, which seemed all the more remarkable since neither fire nor oven was lit. The nearest neighbours were too far away for the aroma to have been of their making.

On another occasion, in the presence of several friends, a smell of roasting meat arose. This appeared to have as little foundation in fact as the earlier manifestation.

Two later occupants, Mr and Mrs Hilliard, also encountered strange smells in the house, although that of baking bread was not among them. Mr Hilliard was unable to identify the smell, referring to it only as 'strange'. It was not strange to his wife, however. Mrs Hilliard, having been brought up in Roman Catholic schools, recognised it at once as the smell of incense.

The couple noticed the perfume about six times in all during their occupancy of the house, and apparently the smell lasted only a minute or so on each occasion.

From time to time, also, footsteps were heard in the building, and on each occasion in the early evening. The Hilliards were very happy in the house and were unworried by the manifestations.

Since they left John o' Lydgate's, the building has been further modernised and central heating installed. I have no information regarding subsequent manifestations, so it seems that this is one more case of disturbance of the material surroundings dislocating or discontinuing the pattern of haunting.

During researches for this book, I have found that persons with one story to tell often know of a second or third. Such was the case with Mrs Elaine Burke of Kessingland, who first told me of the lorry-driver's experience on Blythburgh Common.

Until a few months ago, the Burkes had as near neighbour an elderly man who lived alone. In the manner of lonely old people, he spent a considerable time standing at his gate watching the world go by – and on the off-chance of having a chat with any friendly soul who had time for him. Dennis and Elaine Burke had time for him, and the old fellow was a frequent visitor to their home.

He died some months ago, and the Burkes, who had been fond of him, felt a sense of loss. Elaine had been accustomed to look across from her window and wave to the figure standing by the gate opposite. From time to time after his death she still glanced across, out of habit; and on two such occasions she saw the old man standing, as he had always stood – beside his gateway, waiting.

On each occasion it was a few seconds before the truth dawned on her; that she was seeing not what was present, but what was past.

On the second occasion when she rang me to talk about ghosts, the story had progressed a stage further. Her husband Dennis, had gone into the garage that very evening, to get something from the car. He had been inside the car, when he thought someone entered the garage. He looked up and found the old man standing by the car door. The latter said in the broad Suffolk which had been his natural tongue, 'Now, owd boy, what're y'doin'?' This was the very phrase he had used in real life when coming over to see Dennis Burke.

The figure disappeared in the time it took Dennis to realise that the old man could not possibly be standing where he saw him. The living man retired indoors, upset and shaken by the experience.

Since this occurrence I have had no further reports from Kessingland. It will be interesting to see how long the manifestations continue. With this type of happening, the supernatural appearances may be quite numerous for a short while after death, with strong and detailed manifestations. They usually become weaker and less frequent with the passage of time, and eventually fade entirely. This seems to point to at least a temporary survival of personality after death. It may, of course, be more than temporary.

I have kept one of the most intriguing Suffolk stories to the last.

A friend of mine, Mrs Margaret Morris, bought a cottage some time ago near the town of Halesworth. At one time it must have been two cottages, but the modernisers moved them around a little and made one good-sized dwelling out of the pair. Margaret fell in love with the place, bought it and moved in. She chose to sleep in a bedroom which appeared to be in the older part of the house.

Not long afterwards, she began to experience a recurrent dream, and one of its interesting features was that it only occurred when she slept in this particular bedroom. (Although I am using the past tense in describing the occurrence, the dream, in fact, is still very much in evidence.)

On each occasion she saw two children standing beside her bed. They were aged about seven and four, the girl being the elder. They were dressed in smocks and had a well-brushed and scrubbed look, with their hair freshly combed. Both children, according to Margaret Morris, looked at her as though she ought not to be lying where she was. Their look was one of doubt and puzzlement.

When she told me the story, we talked about it at some length. She was able to give an accurate description of the children's appearance, and she assured me that they always looked the same – 'as though they had been properly washed and dressed by someone, for a special occasion'. And they always stood by the bed and stared unwaveringly at her.

It seemed to me that this was a repetition of some action – possibly one charged with emotion – which had engaged the children in real life. From the description it sounded as though they were cottagers' children; from the pattern of behaviour, one thing suggested itself with considerable force. They were standing by that bed for a specific purpose. 'Could they,' I asked Mrs Morris, 'have been regarding a dead person – perhaps their mother?' She looked flatteringly startled. 'Yes,' she said, with vehemence. 'That's precisely the way they would have looked – the way they do look. They look at me as though I were dead and they can't understand it.'

Again, deduction based on guesses but lacking any historical fact on which to work, it is the best one can do.

The last time I talked with Margaret Morris – about a month ago – I asked if she had seen the children again.

She had. But in another bedroom of the house. And for the first time they had not stood by her bedside. They had not even looked at her. They had been playing in the middle of the room, and were neither tidy nor well-scrubbed;

they behaved like ordinary children of that age, tousled and untidy and completely oblivious of anything outside their play.

It seems the children go with the house, and once lived there. A play-pattern has been hammered into the surroundings and an emotion-pattern. A continual recurrence and a single occurrence, but both are now repeated.

So far only Margaret has seen them, and she is still half-convinced that she dreams what she sees.

I find these children of the past as mesmeric as Henry James's 'Innocents'; and far more attractive. Who were they? And why have their patterns clung when those of their family adults have vanished?

Two more questions in a long chain of unanswerables.

Suffolk is packed with tales, and most of them have a grace and mystery about them which are not always evidenced by ghost stories. Of them all my favourites are the little maid of Sutherland House, and the Watching Children. Perhaps because of the youth of the participants – though it may be that all three of the living beings whose wraiths are now seen, lived to a good age before leaving the material world. It seems to be the moment of emotion which is preserved, or the strongest repetitive behaviour pattern. Biographically progressive history is *not* recorded in the form known as 'supernatural'.

# HUNTINGDONSHIRE
## Love Letters, a Bridge and the Life of Cromwell's Cavalry

Huntingdonshire people still refer to their county as fenland, although there is little now to remind the stranger that this agricultural landscape was once submerged beneath the great fen waters. The reed beds are gone, and the ubiquitous waterways; the wildfowl and the men who lived by shooting them. You could travel miles now before you would find a punt on the rivers and farther still before you'd see a punt-gun, that huge and formidable piece of weaponry.

The fens today are docile, tamed, domestic and peaceful, their acres uncontoured except for an occasional small mound which once stood above the surrounding waters.

Stand on such a knoll now, and it is not difficult to imagine the cattle swimming across from one islet to another seeking pasture, as they did two hundred years ago. Not difficult either, to conjure the reed-rustle as the old fen-tigers poled their boats along the hidden channels, stalking unwary duck or seeking the place where a great pike lurked.

The fen-tigers were no ordinary breed of men. The lives they lived were closer to nature than those of most of their countrymen of the same period. They lived on and by the water and its creatures – water-hen pie was a not unheard-of delicacy and sparrow pudding a commonplace. Whatever swam or flew around the fen was fair game, though 'game' was not a word they would have used when their livelihood depended on what they caught. The fen was work and play, home and recreation. Its conditions were hard and it bred a hard, formidable people. Hereward the Wake and Oliver Cromwell were men of the fens in their day, though not the working fishing-and-shooting fenmen of the peasantry.

Perhaps the inaccessibility of their native lands bred a suspicion of strangers and a dislike of interference by outsiders. Perhaps the constant struggle with a hostile environment stoked the violence lying deep at the root of the East Anglian nature. Whatever the reasons, suspicion and fear were both aroused when drainage of the fens began in the eighteenth century.

To the fenman drainage did not mean land reclaimed from the waters, on which good crops could grow; he saw it only as the loss of his living and his inherited way of life. Men who had always subsisted on the fish and fowl of the waterways found themselves about to be deprived of their ancient rights, and of the very mode of existence which made them what they were. Like the Lincolnshire men in an earlier century, they resisted change and resisted violently.

As fast as the engineers constructed sluice gates and drains to control the spreading waters, these were blown up, demolished or otherwise sabotaged. 'Collaborators' and men working on the schemes were attacked and sometimes murdered. The fenmen considered they were fighting for their rights against invaders and oppressors. All men to them were foreigners who were not fenmen.

But violent times passed. The fens were drained, and the old tigers became farmhands and smallholders. The new-won lands blossomed and were fruitful. Gradually the ways of the water-dwellers faded until they were almost forgotten.

Huntingdonshire's eastern area is true fenland in history and feeling, though farther west the land begins to roll, and give the impression of having been farmland these many centuries. Cromwell himself was a farmer, though this did not prevent him from bringing his own brand of spoliation and violence to the area.

Indeed, whatever in the country does not remind you of the fenland reminds of the Civil War. The area was strongly Parliamentarian, and the few local Royalists must have needed to lie very low in order to stay alive.

It is inevitable that the hauntings should reflect both aspects of the country's history. Many of the stories I found here were seventeenth century in origin; one or two went back to even earlier times, to the days when monasteries and convents supplied the nucleus of rural society. Occasionally a haunting, though belonging to a particular period, was not related in detail to that period, but was domestic or personal in nature.

One such was the haunting of The Red House, Offord Darcy. Offord Darcy and Offord Cluny are neighbouring villages of considerable antiquity; Darcy dating back at least as far as the thirteenth century, and I suspect with Norman or even earlier beginnings. Cluny derived its title from the French abbey with which an estate in the village was associated. It certainly acquired its name in the early days of the Conquest, and the Cluniac monks who resided at Offord stayed for over three hundred years.

The Red House is a mellow and beautiful building and its comparatively youthful exterior is belied the moment one crosses the threshold. Its mellowness is the result of age, its beauty the result of care and taste. Its owners, Mr and Mrs Harold Brown, have lived in the place for 45 years, and have never once seen a ghost. Or I should say *the* ghost. For the previous owners were very much aware of not being the only occupants of the house.

Probably the Browns would have remained ignorant of the haunting, had they not received a call from some visiting Australians, who were curious to see the place in which their own family had once lived. They told the Browns a strange story.

In the eighteenth century the house was owned by people named Morton who were small farmers, but comfortably off. Their daughter fell in love with a man of whom the parents disapproved, and the latter would not countenance any marriage between the two young people. The girl was forbidden to see the man again. Whether she honoured the prohibition or not, it is impossible to know. What is known in that the couple exchanged many love letters. These the girl hid under a loose floorboard in her bedroom, in case her parents should discover that the relationship had not been broken, according to their wishes.

In time all the persons concerned in this family drama died, but from time to time later occupants of what had been the girl's bedroom stated that someone walked into the room in the middle of the night. Many guests complained of this occurrence, but no action was taken by the owners of the house to get rid of their ghost. She seemed a harmless manifestation and they were accustomed now to thinking of the place as haunted.

Then the resident family (named Cawcutt) decided to emigrate to Australia. There was a great packing and sorting and disposing of accumulated impedimenta in the old house, and during the course of it the Cawcutt children, a lively bunch, found a loose floorboard in the guest room. They prised it up, and in the cavity discovered a bundle of letters tied with ribbon and addressed to a Miss Morton. The name meant nothing to them and the contents even less. They were apparently love letters and the children found them very dull. They burned the whole bunch. And from that day onward the ghost of Miss Morton has not disturbed the rest of visitors to The Red House. The Browns seemed a little regretful. For my part, I regretted the casual destruction of fascinating documents of human and historical interest. One doesn't find a packet of eighteenth-century letters every day. I wonder if the Cawcutt children had their bottoms smacked . . .

The interesting feature of this haunting is that the manifestation continued just so long as the love letters remained in existence. Once these were destroyed, the haunt-pattern also disappeared. Coincidence? Or a further proof of a material transmitter as the activating force?

Offord Darcy drifts effortlessly into Offord Cluny. They are one village although divided into two parishes. Cluny also has a ghost – that of an elderly lady who appears in the Manor House.

The house is owned by Lieut-Colonel and Mrs O. N. D. Sismey, and the place has been occupied by members of the same family since 1782, although the house was built as early as 1704.

Shortly after the building was completed, the then owner, Mr Deane, brought home his bride, a Miss Sismey, who appears to have become devoted to the house in which she spent her married life. When Mr Deane died, the property passed to his wife, and she in turn willed it to a Sismey nephew. Since then it seems that when each generation of Sismey men brings home a new bride, the figure of a small, elderly woman appears to the girl. The apparition is said to be that of the first bride to live in the house, Mrs Deane.

The ghost was seen by Colonel Sismey's mother shortly after she first came to the Manor House. Her husband was a solicitor with a London practice and his work frequently kept him in the city for most of the week. On one occasion when he returned home, his young wife told him that she had had a strange experience. One evening while she was reading in the drawing-room, the figure of an elderly woman passed her, and then immediately disappeared. Her husband thought she must momentarily have fallen asleep and had a fleeting dream. However, years afterwards, his own mother mentioned the matter and said that his grandmother had often seen the little old lady.

Apparently the apparition has been seen by at least four generations of Sismey brides – the colonel's great-grandmother, grandmother, mother and wife. For the present Mrs Sismey also encountered the ghost when she was newly married. She describes the ghostly lady as 'charming and benevolent, and seemingly only wanting to assure the bride that she will be happy in the house'. Her appearance seems to constitute a kind of psychic handing-over-of-keys ceremony to the newcomer.

The present Mrs Sismey is now only concerned to know whether or not the ghost will appear to the next generation, for the children of the present owners are daughters. The next Sismey bride may well be the wife of the colonel's grandson. It is not known yet whether the ghost appears only to those bearing the name of Sismey – a name which the little old lady herself brought into the family.

The welcoming apparition appears only in the drawing-room of the Manor House, and has not been seen elsewhere in the building.

The Offords are not far from St Neots and there are a number of stories of hauntings in that neighbourhood. Several of these concern public-houses, among them the Royal Oak at St Neots.

In November 1963, the then landlord and his wife, a Mr and Mrs Hart, underwent a singularly unnerving experience. It was noticed that whenever the landlord went into the old part of the building, an unpleasant smell attached itself to him. It remained with him just so long as he stayed in that part of the house and disappeared as soon as he left it.

Previous tenants had had disturbing experiences in the building, and had needed to resort to exorcism – which cannot have been totally effective, if the troubling of Mr Hart is anything to go by.

Finally, the unpleasantness became thoroughly unnerving, and a team of investigators was called in to hold a séance in the public bar. The result of this was the investigators' discovery that a suicide had taken place in the older part of the building, a man apparently having hanged himself from a meat-hook. According to the psychic research team, the body had not been discovered for three days. The odour which attached itself to Mr Hart and which proved so repugnant was that of a decaying corpse.

I have given here the discoveries of the psychic research team as reported in the local paper shortly after the séance. I know of no form of written proof of the origin of the haunting.

Another haunted hostelry is reputed to be the New Inn at St Neots. Again it is the more ancient part of the building which is affected. Apparently Parliamentarian forces used the place as a billet during the Civil War and it is thought that the Royalist Kimbolton Castle was stormed from St Neots. Local tradition also has it that the Earl of Holland was imprisoned here and several of his officers executed near the building; the Earl's own life ended on the block at the Tower.

In 1963 the licensees were a Mr and Mrs Kerr, and the lady averred that on several occasions she had seen a tall slender man, wearing an ankle-length cloak, standing in the bar. The first time he appeared was about 12.15 a.m., after the bars had closed and the hoteliers had returned to their private quarters. Mrs Kerr came downstairs to make coffee, and saw the figure of a cloaked man walk across the bar through a vestibule door and out into the yard. She followed him into the yard, and then stopped abruptly as realisation dawned on her. She had had to *unbolt* the door into the yard; the figure had apparently *walked straight through it*. Mrs Kerr was naturally upset.

It seems that once or twice visitors to the hotel about this time remarked on their unease when passing a certain spot in the bar. The reader will not be surprised to learn that it was the place where the cloaked figure usually materialised.

A year after the St Neots hauntings a ghost was reported at the old gate house to Paxton Hall. At that time a Mr and Mrs Lloyd and their teenage son, Lindsey, occupied the premises; it was the latter who reported having seen 'a tall man with bushy sideboards, a stovepipe hat and a face resembling that of Abraham Lincoln'. He was seen in two of the bedrooms, and was thought to have been a former schoolmaster who once resided at Paxton Hall. One bedroom in particular always exuded a smell of stale cigars. The door of this room was heavy and solid and closed firmly. However, no matter how decisively it was shut, it invariably opened again within minutes.

These were not the only manifestations. From time to time banging sounds could be heard from this room. The family's cat also showed an aversion to the room, refusing to enter it. A former owner shared the animal's dislike and would not go into this bedroom at all.

Apart from the Lloyds' own live cat, it seems that a ghost cat kept the old schoolteacher company, for several times Mrs Lloyd felt a cat spring on to her bed and walk around, purring. When she put on the light there was no cat present.

A visiting plumber had a distressing time, too. He left his tools on the landing after fixing a recalcitrant water tank, while he went downstairs to work. He was not happy a few minutes later to see his tools roll down the stairs to him one by one. It is said that he departed hastily with his equipment.

I called at the old gate house recently, but the place appeared to be deserted. Perhaps the Lloyds eventually left their spectral lodger and his cat in sole occupation.

There is no doubt that the St Neots area has a considerable number of ghosts. Eynesbury is said to be haunted by the ghost of a former witch, Nanny Izzard, who was expelled by her home village of Great Paxton. Legend states that on certain nights she flies around the area on the traditional broomstick.

Another story of the proverbial type is that of the 'Huntingdonshire Fairy Morgana'. This is a quite incomprehensible tale of the appearance of ghostly troops near St Neots in 1820. It seems that the spectral army also materialised in 1743. The title of the legend seems nonsensical, since the Fairy Morgana is undoubtedly our old mythological friend, Morgan-le-Fay of the Arthurian legend. Morgan-le-Fay or Fand or Vivien, by tradition was the paramour and eventually the destroyer of Merlin – which story incidentally bears some resemblance to the biblical one of Samson and Delilah. How the appearance of a phantom army can be linked with the treacherous Morgan, it is difficult to see. In any case, there are no twentieth-century reports, as far as I know, of the ghost battalions appearing, and I think both this and the previous tale are local legends of a folk nature rather than true hauntings.

Although psychic phenomena appear to be more frequent near or within buildings, a small proportion occurs in open country, or at least out-of-doors. The ghosts of Blythburgh Common have already been noted. Another example occurred in the 1920s, when a local Huntingdonshire man was in wooded country between Eltisley and Yelling in the early hours of one Sunday morning. It seems an unusual time to have been abroad, and one can only assume that the man was returning home late from a Saturday night shindig. The night was exceptionally quiet, with that particular quality of stillness which is almost tangible. Without warning, the peace was shattered by a banging and rattling which resembled nothing so much as the sound of moving chains. The sounds were only about twenty feet away, but the man could see no light or movement in the place from which the noise emanated.

More curious than frightened, for he was convinced that the rational explanation was that someone had been wood-cutting, probably illicitly, he returned to the spot the next day. There was no sign that anything untoward had taken place; certainly no sign of tree-felling.

It happened that this man had a friend living at Kimbolton who frequently went shooting in the woods of that area. This second man also heard what he thought were rattling chains within the woodland, and he was sufficiently alarmed to foreswear the woods as a shooting area afterwards. Here again the sounds had seemed very near the listener, but nothing at all was to be seen.

A haunting nearer in time occurred about ten years ago, and was reported by the *Cambridge News.*

Three people were motoring along the A14 road between Caxton and Huntingdon one night, and were in the neighbourhood of the turning to Graveley, when they noticed a marked drop in temperature inside the car. So abrupt was the onset of the cold that the driver stopped the car. All three of the vehicle's occupants felt that a fourth presence had joined them.

A few days later one of the three, a young woman, awoke to find the figure of a man standing by her bedside. She first noted his black frock coat and top hat, and then his gleaming teeth as he grinned at her before disappearing.

The other two occupants of the car also had peculiar experiences immediately following the drive, as a result of which all three decided to retrace their route along the A14 a few nights later.

Again the sequence of events was similar. As they approached the Graveley turn a sudden fall in temperature occurred. There is no record of any subsequent hauntings, but the victims of this particular one concluded that whatever they had picked up in the car the first night had followed them home. An unnerving aspect of the affair was that the materialisation resembled an undertaker.

Who was this ghostly hitch-hiker, and why were these three people the only motorists to collect the phantom? Ghosts of undertakers, in popular mythology, are usually thought to be harbingers of death, much in the way that falling mirrors and pictures, white pigeons, howling dogs or a bouquet of red and white flowers are death-prophecies. There is no record in this case of any fatality occurring to or near-missing these particular motorists.

One of the best known stories of haunting in the County of Huntingdon is that of the Nun's Bridge at Hinchingbrooke. The earliest written version as far as I know (and for this I am indebted to Mr Michael Deaves of Comberton, Cambridge) occurs in a book appearing in 1874. It is a versified, and I would guess much distorted version of the tale of a girl with whom St Benedict fell in love. The poem is pure doggerel and not worth reprinting in full. Its only value is that it describes the exact location of the haunting.

Near the birthplace of Cromwell you may see to this day
The remains of a house which is haunted they say,
At the foot of a hill near a small winding lane
And here I have heard this sad murder occurred,
Yes this is the place where the lovers were slain.

Other versions of the legend say that the girl was a nun and her lover a monk. Certainly the nearby Hinchingbrooke House was once a convent. Local history states that a large priory also existed in the neighbourhood, and that some traffic took place between the two.

From this point the story slides into folklore. According to local tradition, the young lovers used the bank of the Alconbury stream near Hinching-brooke bridge as their rendezvous. They were discovered, and both put to death for their sin. Nothing has been seen of the man, but the spirit of the young nun is said to appear on or near the bridge, occasionally accompanied by the figure of an older woman dressed as a nurse.

The last recorded instance I can find of the sighting of the apparition was in 1965, when a Mrs Valerie Bain of Huntingdon was driving with her husband from that town towards Brampton. As they approached the bridge they saw upon it the figure of a nun; almost immediately there appeared beside her a second form, wearing the dress of a nurse.

The Bains had been intending to spend some time in Brampton, but in fact decided against it and returned to Huntingdon again shortly afterwards by way of the bridge. They might have expected this time to cross without seeing anything unusual, but again the two apparitions materialised, and on this occasion the nurse seemed to be laughing. Mrs Bain, not surprisingly, screamed.

On my visit to Huntingdonshire I came upon Nun's Bridge by chance, and in fact had crossed the new bridge which carries a good modern trunk road across the stream, before I noticed the second, much older version. It stood to the left of the new road, and the lane it carried, which had once been the main highway, now is used as a lay-by.

I was not sure of my whereabouts, but all the descriptions I had read of Hinchingbrooke fitted this place; the little lane, the trees crowding down to the stream, the ancient bridge, the gloomy, green-grey light near the water – and the suggestion of a great house hidden behind the trees and high fences.

I stopped the car, got out and looked around. Sure enough a sign said that these were the Hinchingbrooke grounds, and this the mysterious bridge of the story. I walked across it and down to the stream. Bright sunlight on the bridge, a Corot-like shimmer of silver-green on the stream banks. No ghosts; only a sense of the place being set apart in time, being utterly distinct from its brash modern counterpart which conducted the swingeing traffic into Huntingdon. It must have been secluded and beautiful once, before the arrival of the insatiable motor-car.

This is a story in which several different elements are brought together by the various versions and one is in some difficulty to find the truth.

On the one hand the ghost is that of a local girl, her lover (who has never haunted the area) is St Benedict; both were murdered by the girl's brother. On the other hand the girl is a nun and her lover a monk, and their manner of death is not stated. The ghostly nurse is unexplained in both versions. The

*Nun's Bridge, Hinchingbrooke*

researcher may choose which tale he believes. I prefer the second. Adjacent nunnery and priory could well have given rise to a love affair; such occurrences were not uncommon. The lovers may have been unfortunate in contracting their alliance at a time when church matters were being handled strictly. At such periods punishment was severe. There were other eras in history when the holy orders were less obedient to the laws of Poverty, Chastity and Obedience, and violations were condoned or ignored. The climate of public opinion was as variable in the Middle Ages, though within a smaller compass, as it is now. The Hinchingbrooke pair were unlucky.

I heard it said in Huntingdon town that the large number of accidents near Hinchingbrooke bridge are due to the haunting. Local people are still reluctant to walk over it after dark.

Another tale states that a ghostly drummer has been heard beating a tattoo in the bridge's neighbourhood, but I understand that the drummer in question was a substantial Air Force gentleman from a nearby RAF station. Having learned the genuine ghost story, he decided to create one of his own, and borrowing a drum, he marched up and down the banks of Alconbury brook, drumming deep into the night. As far as I know, he was neither haunted for his impertinence, nor prosecuted for disturbing the peace.

Hinchingbrooke House was once the home of the Earl of Sandwich, whose portrait and story are associated with Sutherland House in Southwold noted in an earlier chapter. Part of the house's foundations are those of the old convent, the new structure being erected in the time of Charles I. To tie up another strand in the web, Oliver Cromwell is said to have played there when a boy. The house is now in use as a school.

Another monastic ghost is alleged to haunt a modern house in Hemingford Abbots. He is known to the occupants as 'Brother Dominic', and all they see of him is a shadowy figure. The house is built next to the church, and the area must certainly have been abbey property in pre-Reformation days, so a haunting monk is well within the bounds of possibility.

Sometimes there is no clue to the origin of a haunting, and occasionally even no indication of the actual haunter. Action occurs, but it is the movement of material objects only, and although these movements may follow a pattern, the originator of the pattern may not be apparent. Such seems to have been the case in The Crown Inn at Great Staughton. The events took place towards the end of 1970.

The occurrences were varied and of a mischievous, though not violent nature. The then landlords were a Mr and Mrs Green, who took over the licence at the end of 1970. Shortly after moving in, they encountered a series of strange events. Clothing disappeared, to turn up later in a different place; bottles clinked together in the bar after the family had gone to bed; a radio turned itself on, apparently without human assistance. On another occasion when Mrs Green expressed a disbelief in ghosts to a customer an electric clock fixed above the bar shot off the wall with some violence.

No explanation was ever put forward for these happenings, and although it was known that the pub was over two hundred years old, the Greens knew no details of its history, and were therefore unable to make any guess regarding the nature of their visitant.

Certain of these activities sound poltergeist-like. However, this is one case of insufficient evidence being available to point to any solution of the mystery.

The triangular area of St Neots, Huntingdon and St Ives holds some of the best ghost stories in the county. Many of these are historical in origin, several are associated with ancient buildings, and a few relate to private houses. The one place where I did not expect to find a ghost story was in a newspaper office. Gentlemen of the Press are usually a little sceptical of anything which cannot actually be photographed or persuaded to give them an interview. However, they are sensitive to the unusual and quick to react to it.

I had found the *Cambridge Evening News* staff most helpful, both in Cambridge and at their Huntingdon office when I had consulted their files. It was with some surprise, though, that I learned they possessed a ghost of their own. The staff were reluctant to fix a definite label on the occurrences which had taken place in their office at Huntingdon, but when these were described, it seemed that this was yet another psychic manifestation of the footsteps-and-doors variety.

The office building is a converted Georgian house, with parts dated earlier. A modern façade has been grafted on to fit the newspaper image, but the rest of the building has been well preserved and little touched. The second storey of the building is in use as a flat and is traditionally occupied by one of the reporters.

The present incumbent, Mr Kellaher, said he had many times heard noises of doors opening and closing when the building was empty. On investigation he had found nothing to account for the sounds. One door in particular, leading to a cellar, adjoins the downstairs kitchen. The door fits firmly into its frame, and considerable manual pressure is required to open it. However, one night when the reporter was in the kitchen, his back turned to the cellar, he heard the door open behind him. When he looked round, he found it standing ajar.

The previous occupant of the flat suffered from deafness, but he, too, had heard unexplained noises in the house, and the sound of doors being opened and shut. Other members of the staff have heard footsteps, and on one occasion the sound of someone walking along a passageway. In each case when the noises were investigated, there appeared to be no cause for them.

There is a local rumour that a servant girl was murdered in the building in the days when the house was privately owned and occupied. Perhaps the sounds are an echo of her occupation, though why they should take so dull and ordinary a pattern, when they might well have echoed whatever tragedy overtook her, I cannot imagine.

It was in Huntingdon that I heard stories of hauntings at Buckden, a pleasant village lying near the auto-artery of the A1. Originally known as Bugeden, it is mentioned in the Domesday survey. At one time the village lay within the diocese of Lincoln and formed a stopping place on the main north–south route. Predictably, two coaching inns sprang up astride the road, to supply long-distance travellers with fresh teams of horses. The pubs stand there still, islands in time, The George on one side, The Lamb on the other, both handsome specimens of their period. One listens in vain for the sound of great wheels rattling in over the cobbles, of coachmen's whips slicing the air, for the snort and stamp of horses, and the nostalgic ring of metal from the local smithy. There is no longer need of a smithy in Buckden for the roaring mail coach days have receded. No local gentry ride in, and the fugitive highwayman no longer makes for The George as a place of refuge.

*Buckden Palace*

Did he ever? There is a long standing legend in Huntingdonshire that Dick Turpin used this hotel. Some people even speak of his ghost haunting the inn. When I called there and talked with the landlord the story seemed unlikely to have much foundation. True, there is a room known as Turpin's room. (Significantly, the other rooms all bear the names of English monarchs.) There is also a black oak hatch built into the outside wall of the corridor directly opposite the door of that room, supposedly as an emergency exit for the highwayman when pursuit was hot. The story is another local tradition which probably had some foundation in fact. However, that fact is now so remote, its detail so ill-recorded, that only the verbally inherited tale remains, like a dream recollected on awakening, which grows fainter as the day progresses, until by mid-afternoon nothing is remembered save that some dream occurred.

As for the ghost, the landlord knew of none, though his wife had occasionally been disturbed by the falling of sundry items from a shelf in the bar. It seems this had happened several times when no human agency could have effected the occurrences. Insufficient evidence, I think, for a haunting.

The Lamb opposite has a magnificent wheel-hub ceiling and an inglenook fireplace, which on the day I called was vigorously puffing out smoke into the room. 'Way of the wind,' said the landlord resignedly. 'We are trying to cure it.' If he'd tried that in the pub's early days he'd have been arrested for witchcraft.

Buckden has an air of clinging desperately to its seclusion, for though it was once on the main London post-highway, and now is not, the sense of encroachment is stronger now than it can ever have been. The A1 is so near that the low murmur of fast-travelling traffic underscores all the village's activities. New estates are creeping round, industry spreading like fungus. Buckden, sleepy and historic, waits for what is to come.

A rearguard action is being fought, however. Buckden Palace or Buckden Towers as it is known locally, was once a seat of the Bishops of Lincoln, and some interesting bits of English history were enacted there. It was visited by, among others, Thomas Wolsey, then Bishop of Lincoln, the formidable Margaret Beaufort, mother of Henry VII, and by Henry VIII with his fifth wife, Catherine Howard.

However, Buckden Palace's chief claim to fame seems to be that for a year it housed Catherine of Aragon, Henry VIII's first queen. Confined here at Henry's orders after the dissolution of her marriage, the Queen received so much local sympathy and affection that Henry feared she would become a focus for treasonable plotting, and tried to have her removed to a safer area. The Duke of Suffolk was sent to Buckden to effect the removal, but Catherine was not to be intimidated. She refused to accept either Fotheringhay or Somersham as an alternative to Buckden, and finally shut herself in her room and locked the door against Suffolk's shouted and ill-tempered threats.

The people of Buckden gathered outside the Palace, armed with scythes and billhooks, waiting belligerently for Suffolk and his men to attempt to move the Queen by force. The Duke took stock of the situation and retired defeated. All he could do was to take away from Catherine those few furnishings she had brought from London, and to imprison some of her English servants. The Queen herself stayed in her locked room until her tormentor had returned to his master.

In the following May Catherine was finally moved to Kimbolton, where she remained until her death in 1536.

*Kimbolton Castle*

Buckden Palace is owned now by the Claretian Missionaires, a Spanish monastic order, whose members are engaged in restoring the fine old building to something approaching its original state. The monks deny any certain knowledge of a ghost in the palace, but there is a strong local tradition that Catherine of Aragon has been seen in the small room behind the chapel. When I visited it, this room was cold, but no more so than you would expect of any building of that age – and certainly no more so than other rooms in the Palace through which I passed.

I did not enter Kimbolton Castle, which was the last home of Henry's sad, rejected queen. Catherine died there on 7 January 1536, perhaps of cancer, perhaps of poisoning. Her former husband donned a bright yellow suit and gave a ball at Greenwich to celebrate the occasion.

It is said that Catherine has been seen at Kimbolton also, but I found no one who could confirm the story.

There is also a tale that a child was flung from a balcony here into the courtyard, and that the haunting is connected with this incident rather than with the death of the old queen. Again I found no confirmation. All was rumour, rumour. Kimbolton had its time of history and drama, when Catherine's faithful supporters tried to gain access to her and were denied admittance; when the cavaliers of Chapuys's train sang Spanish songs to her and her women from the wrong side of the moat; when Chapuys, the Imperial Spanish Ambassador, sent his jester to fool and tumble in an effort to cheer their fenland imprisonment for a few hours. But these scenes are deep buried in the past, and there is no certain evidence that they are or have been repeated in any psychic manifestation. Kimbolton holds its old secrets, a country place in what was once a wild, secluded landscape.

In the hundred years which separated the mid-sixteenth from the mid-seventeenth centuries, the face and quality of English life changed. The Tudors had vanished and with them a whole way of life and thought; the Stuarts had reigned, departed, and were about to return again. England had suffered a regicide, a Civil War; and a decade of intense and fanatical Puritanism. Churches had been desecrated in the name of pure, reformed religion; old Royalist houses had been burned, or occasionally occupied by Parliamentary troops and treated in the way that soldiers' billets are usually treated.

Whether the Old Rectory at Eynesbury was ever a Royalist house, I do not know. In a county so staunchly supporting the Parliament's cause, a Royalist Rector would afford an irresistible challenge to Parliamentary billeting officers. According to historical records, one Thomas Barton was presented with the living by Charles I in the year 1629, later leaving to become Rector of Westmeston in Sussex, of which living he was later deprived because of his Royalist sympathies. During the Civil War, this cleric was Chaplain to Prince Rupert, and in 1660 he was restored to the living at Westmeston. John Turner became incumbent at Eynesbury in 1649, but much of the period between these incumbencies remains unaccounted for. However, in view of certain aspects of the Old Rectory itself and of various manifestations which occurred there until the year 1969, it seems likely that the premises were in use during the Civil War as a billet for Parliamentary cavalry.

*The Old Rectory, Eynesbury*

Eynesbury is an older parish even than nearby St Neots, and according to local records, there has been a rectory there since 1410. The whole building is still in occupation, but it is the older part of the house in which the manifestations have occurred, and in the upper rather than the lower floor.

It is a long, low, infinitely pleasing building, with the newer portion of the house on the right of the main entrance. On the left side are traces of a former wall and part of a doorway, and on the south (i.e. left) end of the house an outbuilding which formerly housed a type of boiler. When the present owners, Dr and Mrs Hey, bought the premises in 1967, the boiler was thought to be part of the old wash-house, but an architect employed by them at that time, stated that it had been a component of a forge or kiln. The chimney connected with the boiler was not bonded into the wall of the outbuilding, and was later demolished as being unsafe. No trace was found of any pottery or sherds, and this seemed to dispose of the kiln theory. The possibility remains that it had been part of an ancient forge.

Shortly after the present owners moved into the house, Dr Hey's mother, who lives with her son and his family, began to hear noises in the upper apartments. The sounds varied from that of clanging metal on the landing to the sound of a man's bronchitic cough in the room which she occupied. She also heard the sound of footsteps, and occasionally of ribald laughter and raised voices coming from what had once been the servants' quarters.

I had been intrigued by the letters I received from Mrs Joan Hey, wife of the owner of the house, and was particularly glad to accept her invitation to visit Eynesbury.

Joan Hey, a charming level-headed woman, told me the story of a night in August 1968 when her son, then aged six, who slept in the bedroom nearest to the landing on the old (south) side of the house, had awakened and complained of someone walking about outside his door. His grandmother, whose apartments are on the opposite side of the landing to those of the children and their parents, also heard footsteps. 'Someone walking with heavy shoes or boots on.' She did not think at the time that the sounds were unnatural in origin. She imagined that her son was late retiring and it occurred to her that he was likely to awaken the children.

Dr and Mrs Hey, however, had already retired, though they were not asleep, having been awakened by the child's outcry concerning the footsteps.

About half an hour after the boy had been disturbed (time around 2.30 a.m.) the younger Mrs Hey became apprehensive and then immediately received a distinct impression that a man was standing at the foot of the double bed. The figure wore a dark cloak and a wide-brimmed hat. Neither she nor her husband had previously heard any of the sounds reported by other inmates of the house. And it was not until two or three days after this occurrence, that Dr Hey also mentioned having seen a figure at the bed's foot that night. His impression differed a little from his wife's. He recalled the figure as being male, dark, wearing a wide-brimmed hat, but gowned in a dark brown habit tied with a girdle. Both husband and wife agreed that the shape they had seen was opaque, the face completely shadowed, and the figure unmoving. Their impression was that the representation was of a man in the prime of life, between thirty and forty years old.

Mrs Hey, senior, recounted to me certain interesting experiences of her own which she had previously not discussed for fear of alarming her family.

It appears that on one occasion she was awakened by the sound of falling metal on the landing near the children's rooms. She thought these were objects being tipped from a sack on to the floor, and had the impression (a mental picture, I believe) of pipe joints of a dark metal looking either as if they had come out of the river or as if they were well greased and oiled.

Another time she heard a similar noise during the night and again had a mental picture of the falling objects. On this occasion she thought them to be two in number, cylindrical in shape and possibly made of brass, though the metal appeared greyish in places.

On yet another occasion she awoke to the sounds of digging from the garden behind the house. I say 'garden', but in fact the immediate surroundings of the old building are cobbled, a surface of this nature being the most suitable for horses. Horses were certainly housed here, for their tethering rings are still to be seen fixed to the side of one garden wall.

The digging heard by the old lady continued, and knowing the ground to be cobbled, she was puzzled to account for the noise. Then it occurred to her that what she was hearing was *the sound of the cobbles being laid*. She got up and looked out of her window, but of course nothing unusual was to be seen.

On yet another occasion she heard the sound of heavy furniture being moved about over apparently bare wooden floors. The night she heard the laughter and raised voices must have been particularly unnerving, for the noise was that of men who have been drinking. The idea of a Roundheads' party certainly raises the eyebrows. One has never imagined them a celebratory breed.

There was another time when an elderly guest stayed in the house – a retired schoolteacher of a somewhat nervous disposition. She knew nothing whatever of the Heys' previous experiences and could not have anticipated a disturbed night or yet been aware of the building's history. Her hosts mentioned nothing to her of their own knowledge. The next morning she complained of having been unable to sleep because of the sound of horses and clattering. She asked if there were stables nearby. To the best of the family's knowledge there were not, nor had been within living memory.

So much for the twentieth-century story. Let us now look at this in relation to the house's history.

In the seventeenth century Eynesbury was at the heart of Parliamentary country. The Rectory, however, had been occupied at one time by a Royalist incumbent. Horses had been stabled in the yard and garden, according to the evidence of the tethering rings. This suggests that there were more than two or three animals. The hint of a possible forge at the south end of the house suggests that a smithy existed here. If this were so, then many horses must have been present – possibly a troop of cavalry. The large cobbled areas around the house support this theory. And where better to billet the troopers than in this old house which not only had Royalist connections, but affiliations with the old despised, and in Puritan eyes, unreformed religion? It must be remembered that the Roundheads had a penchant for this kind of protest. Hardly a church in eastern England in which they did not at some time bed down their horses.

So, the cavalry are stationed in the house. Officers or men? Possibly officers in the large upstairs rooms. The apparition seen by Dr and Mrs Hey seems to have worn garments distinguishing him from a trooper.

What of the individual manifestations? Judging by the present plan of the house, and by what clues to its original structure remain outside, it seems likely that an outer (possibly stone) staircase ascended to the second-storey level, and probably found entrance through a door into what is now the Heys' bedroom. This staircase must have had its foot at a point near the smithy, and it could be that a mounting block also was present at this point. The juxtaposition of outside stone stairs and mounting block may still be seen in many old village communities.

There remain the noises heard by the child and his grandmother. Those who ride horses habitually wear boots, and the Cromwellian cavalry were no exception. A booted man does not tread lightly.

It is possible, too, that furniture would be moved over uncarpeted floors when the soldiers first took possession.

However, for me the really interesting feature of these manifestations is neither the cloaked apparition nor the roistering soldiery, but *the sound of metal being tipped from sacks on to the floor.* It was the second manifestation of this kind which most intrigued me.

What manner of brass object would be carried about in sacks? I thought of various accoutrements, but none seemed to the elder Mrs Hey to convey the idea of the noise she had heard. At the moment of hearing the sound, she had had a mental picture of the objects being decanted. They were, she averred, about two and a half feet long, cylindrical and brass – possibly decorated at one end.

The only objects which fitted this description were shell cases, but the seventeenth century was too early in time for this form of ammunition to have been used. It was then brought to my notice by a friend, expert in military history, and himself an historical writer of distinction, that the short cannon of the time fitted the given description. Illustrations of this weapon show a short gun barrel of about the size and shape described by the old lady. Why the gun barrels should have been carried in a sack, and why spilled out upon the floor, it is difficult to see. Old Mrs Hey heard what she heard. She said the metal 'made a terrible noise'; which, if it was a couple of gun barrels, is fairly certain.

All this is surmise, intelligent guessing, if you will. There may perhaps be a better explanation, but so far neither I nor the Hey family have thought of it.

I believe that what the family heard and saw up until the year 1969 was a re-enactment of the most exciting part of the house's history, the time when its occupants were living lives of heightened drama and emotional tension. Patterns were laid down then which appear to have been recorded by the surroundings, and which have been replayed regularly since that time. Until 1969. It was in this year that the Heys had the old tiled roof of the house removed, and replaced by a new, sounder structure. The old roof had superseded an even earlier one of thatch, some time between the years 1607 and 1673.

Since the new roof was completed (in 1970), there has been neither sight, sound nor symptom of any manifestation whatsoever in the Old Rectory. It appears that whatever operated there formerly is no longer able to do so. I think it is unlikely that anything more will be heard of Cromwell's cavalry in that place.

Probably the 'old' – i.e. the first tiled – roof was in position on the house before the Civil War began. And that that roof was the recorder of what went on beneath it seems equally likely. Recorder and transmitter. Now it is gone and the result is a total absence of manifestation. An unhaunted house.

I had the impression that the present occupants regretted the loss of their echoes from the past. Such mirrors and touchstones, though not particularly rare, do yet afford a glimpse of how life was in an earlier age.

Since writing the foregoing, further information has come to light regarding the Old Rectory at Eynesbury, as a result of enquiries made by Mrs Joan Hey.

Mrs Hey approached a daughter of the family who owned the house prior to Dr Hey's purchase of it, and asked if she had noticed anything unusual about the house. The reply was, interesting, and I give a verbatim account of the conversation as Mrs Hey gave it to me.

Q. Have you or has anyone in your family ever had any experiences connected with hauntings in the house?
A. My mother did, but she is of that type.
Q. Well, what exactly did she experience?
A. She wouldn't go to bed alone, or be left alone upstairs at night.
Q. Why was that?
A. She said she had seen a man in the room and he came and stood at the side of the bed. She was transfixed and could not call out or anything.
Q. Can you describe this man?
A. He was dark, wearing an old raincoat and a hat with a brim, about fifty, she said.
Q. That tallies, though my husband and I had the impression of a character, I think, before the time of raincoats. But definitely a dark shadow, in dark clothing and with a hat?
A. Yes, that's right. She was quite definite about the hat and that he came right close to the bed. Mother also used to come in and say she could smell tobacco, though nobody had been in who was smoking.
Q. That's a new one. My husband is a heavy smoker so I doubt if I should notice the smell of tobacco as being anything out of the ordinary. Still you do agree that the hauntings were upstairs rather than down and male in character?
A. Yes, definitely.

Mrs Hey remarks in passing that the parents of the girl slept in the same room as is occupied by her and her husband.

A strange and fascinating story. I half regret the removal of that roof. Heaven knows what other revelations might have come to light about life in the New Model Army.

Occasionally during researches into the so-called 'psychic', the enquirer finds a story of apparent historic interest which yet turns out to be largely fictitious, or, at least garbled.

The Golden Lion Inn at St Ives has been noted for some years for its ghost, but the various facets of the quoted story have a disturbing ring, as though the pieces belonged each to a different tale. In the first place the ghost is said to be that of a woman reputed to have been Oliver Cromwell's mistress. Now if you go, as I did, to the Cromwell museum in Huntingdon and look at the various portraits and the bust of the Lord Protector, you will not have the impression of a sensual man. The face is that of an authoritarian, dedicated, even fanatical personage, with a powerful will and a mind of similar calibre. It is a face, for instance, totally dissimilar in structure and expression from that of Edward Montague, Earl of Sandwich, whose portrait hangs on an adjacent wall. This is that same Earl of Sandwich who stayed in Southwold the night before the battle of Sole Bay; the same earl whose story is interwoven with that of the red-headed servant girl of Sutherland House.

Cromwell's appearance suggests that dalliance with women would not be among his weaknesses. The countenance is closed, shut in, suspicious, single-minded: even these old canvases convey something of the inner power which must have been vigorously present in the paintings' subject.

So the first premise of The Golden Lion's ghost story seems unlikely.

Refutation of the second is based on the fact that the lady's reported psychic activities have not followed a pattern, but appear to have been various and unpredictable. Bells, previously disconnected, were heard ringing; pictures fell from the wall in Room No. 15; a bolted door between Rooms 12 and 14 opened of its own accord; a painting changed colour in Room 14; a guest had the bedclothes stripped from his bed. In fact, most of the recorded occurrences in recent years centred round a young supermarket manager with whom the above incidents are connected. The only sighting of the apparition appears to have been by a boy of thirteen, who came down one night and asked his parents if he could be moved, as he did not like the lady in the strange dress.

The ghost is known locally as the Lady in Green, and the portrait, reputedly of the Puritan woman, which is said to turn green at certain times, was shown to me with considerable pride. It turned out not to be the seventeenth-century canvas I had expected, but a late nineteenth-century piece by Hubert von Herkomer, in the pre-Raphaelite style; an imaginative work with a shadowy, ambiguous expression which could well have given rise to speculation and possibly legend.

Perhaps there was at one time a haunting of The Golden Lion, though I am doubtful about any recent manifestations.

The last place I visited before leaving Huntingdonshire was in the east of the county, good fen country on the Huntingdon/Cambridgeshire border. The Ferry Boat Inn at Holywell is also well known for its ghost story. I had the feeling that the occupants were tired of hearing about the tale, and wished to ignore it and any who enquired of it. My enquiries were directed away from the inn to a house a few yards down the river bank.

Mr Tom Arnold's house is set, like the Ferry Boat, facing the smooth slow waters of the river Ouse. At this point the river is wide, reed-fringed, patrolled by coot, grebe and swan, and in high summer no doubt by pleasure boats also. But this was March – a warm sunny day with the light reflected blue and sharp from the water's surface and blackthorn blossom stitching a white cotton fringe to the bank vegetation. One had to look back at the inn – half-timbered in black and white – to be reminded either of living humanity or its echoes.

The pub was preparing for its Sunday morning influx, so I moved on to call upon Tom Arnold. The latter was engaged in building an upstairs cupboard, but good-humouredly downed tools in order to talk about the Ferry Boat, which he has known and near which he has lived all his life.

After half an hour's conversation it was apparent that this story also possessed contradictory elements. However, certain basic facts stood out, which pointed to a real manifestation.

The local legend is of a lady in white, who walks into the pub and points to a certain flagstone in the floor of the bar. No doubt this tale has been current for a long time, for it appears to have been tricked out with local interpretations. For instance, the phantom's pointing to the flagstone was taken to mean that something must be hidden beneath it. And what would anyone hide under a stone but treasure? In the days when rural communities lived in considerable hardship and poverty, this line of thought was the most attractive and natural. No doubt the flagstone was taken up and nothing found beneath, but this by no means destroyed the legend.

The story was perpetuated and handed down. Mr Arnold remembered his grandparents speaking of it, and even in their day the tale was old.

I asked the obvious question. Tom Arnold lowered his considerable bulk into a chair, then regarded me thoughtfully.

'Something happened one night,' he said, 'which I can't account for.'

He was playing cards in the pub one evening with the then landlord, and was seated with his back to the door. The hour was late, but it was not unusual for the men to sit late over their card game. Without warning, the door at Arnold's back opened, and he heard a man's cough directly behind him. He thought it must be the local policeman, who occasionally called in at that hour. When he glanced round, the door was certainly open, but no one had entered. Assuming the wind to be responsible, he got up and closed the door. The card game continued, but the landlord also had heard the cough and he also thought a man had entered the room.

The Ferry Boat has always been a pub in living memory, though its appearance a century ago was a good deal less venerable than it is now – and that not due to the passage of a mere hundred years. Tom Arnold showed me a faded old photograph of the place at the end of the nineteenth century. It bore no trace then of the black and white half-timbering which now gives it its look of age; a casual glance could easily have mistaken it for a farmhouse.

The spectral woman in white is said to appear on a specific date, 17 March, and to walk along the outside path and into the inn before approaching her flagstone.

*The Ferry Boat Inn, Holywell*

Within recent years a psychical research society became interested in the story, and came down to investigate the phenomenon, bringing with them suitable equipment for the registration of temperature changes, etc. The date chosen was the obvious one, 17 March, and apparently the visit was repeated subsequently on the anniversary of the haunting.

As a result of their researches, the society claimed to have unearthed the following information: the apparition was that of a Juliet Tewsley, who, following an unsuccessful love affair with a woodcutter named Thoms Zowl, committed suicide.

In earlier times, according to Tom Arnold, the Ferry Boat Inn was situated at a crossroads, the river ferry itself presumably linking one part of the road with that on the opposite bank.

Although it was usual for consecrated burials to take place at a crossroads, beneath the sacred cross, such interment was not permitted to suicides. These unfortunates were commonly buried on the highway and not uncommonly with a stake through the heart to prevent wanderings of the unconsecrated spirit; it follows that the girl may have been interred in the neighbourhood of the inn, if not actually within its precincts. Rather than indicating treasure, her pointing finger is more likely to indicate her body's grave. Some such conclusions were reached, I think, by the psychical researchers.

Perhaps the latter's activities were too widely advertised or aroused local animosity or discomfort. Whatever the reason, before the last of their visits a practical joker fixed electrical apparatus under the flagstone and produced a whole series of fascinating and irrelevant phenomena which discouraged the researchers from any further attempt at serious investigation. Since then the white lady has remained undisturbed and as far as I could gather, has not reappeared. The last person to see her died some years ago.

We have, therefore, a story in three parts concerning

(a) A ghostly woman in white, who enters the inn, points to a flagstone and then disappears. The flagstone thought locally to conceal a treasure-cache

(b) A door in the pub which on one occasion opened without warning and the sound of a man's cough heard as he entered. Incident heard by two persons, but apparently never repeated

(c) A detailed story of a named woman (Juliet Tewsley) said to have been a suicide, who could have been buried in the vicinity of the inn. Unverified.

One might assume a connection between (a) and (c), but there is no evidence to suggest that (b) belongs to the same manifestation, though it may, of course, do so.

That, briefly, is the story of the Ferry Boat's ghost. Afterwards Tom Arnold and I discussed what we separately meant by the term haunting. When I spoke of my own belief that incidents are 'recorded' by material objects and 're-broadcast' later, he asked if I believed that Time was an element in such manifestations. I did and do. In fact, Time seems to me to be the key to the enigma. Incidents which occurred in the past are re-played (the time between live incident and psychic manifestation may be anything from a few hours to several centuries), persons who lived in the past, reappear after death or repeat actions which are witnessed by living individuals. In this context chronological – or as Priestley describes it, man-made – Time ceases to function according to the properties we usually attribute to it, and appears to work horizontally. To put it another way, instead of Time operating *in sequence*, with one event following another, the events occur *out* of sequence, as though they moved along parallel conveyor belts, so that Time Past, Time

Present and Time Future become either interchangeable or superimposed one upon another. A similar state to this exists during dreaming or unconsciousness; and this we accept more readily than the encounters with so-called ghosts. I said something of this to Tom Arnold. 'You are talking,' he said, 'of Einstein's Relativity Theory.'

The Time Theory continued to plague me for some hours after I left Holywell. And all the way back through the blackthorn-blossomed lanes and silvery March sunlight I wondered what Time is and why we understand it so little. Perhaps the very car I drove was, at that moment, registering its shape upon surrounding space and time, to reappear in Time ahead and print itself upon the disbelieving retina of someone yet unborn.

A thought to chasten human arrogance.

# CAMBRIDGESHIRE
### A Watchman, A Poltergeist and the Rattling Thing in the Coalhouse

In the relationship of counties, Cambridgeshire is first cousin to Huntingdon-shire. It has the same open skies, the same slow full rivers and much of the same reticence and depth in its people. Both counties are part of the old fenland and in spite of the twentieth century have managed to retain a quality of aloofness which is at once attractive and baffling.

Such differences as exist seem to be ones of influence. Cambridgeshire is vitally aware of its ancient town and university. Everywhere there appear to be connections with the colleges, either through the latter's landholdings or because of historical ties. Huntingdonshire is seemingly without this central hub, functioning in smaller units, de-centralised.

So to look at any aspect of Cambridgeshire, it is necessary first to consider its county town. And it is a beautiful town, looking in upon itself, admiringly, wonderingly, critically; a self-confident town, secure in its record of achievement. Its history is almost as old as English history, though less diverse.

But if you expect to find rich gleanings in the occult field you will be disappointed. Perhaps the soil is too well-nourished by ideas to support the scientifically unprovable ghost. Certainly I found little in the town of Cambridge to suggest that any of it was haunted, though a local inhabitant confirmed that the colleges had their ghosts.

'They have them, all right,' he said, 'they just don't recognise them. Or if they do, they don't intend to talk about them.'

And so it proved. The only ghost I heard of in the colleges was one thought to haunt Corpus Christi. Allegedly the ghost of an old proctor, it is said to walk along one of the corridors. However, the original corridor in the building was at a different level from the modern version and the apparition is therefore displaced in relation to its new surroundings – that is, it walks as during lifetime, at the old floor level, two feet above that of the new.

This kind of displacement phenomenon is interesting when considered in relation to the transmission-of-image theory. Presupposing that the 'transmitter' remains *in situ* over the intervening time from the original incident to the present day, it should continue to relay its information – in the case of the Corpus ghost, an image – to precisely the same place on the 'screen' (i.e. the material surroundings) as the image occupied in actual life. Should the screen be partially obstructed, as it would be by the raising of a floor level or blocking up of a door; or extended by the lowering of a floor level, the position of the image would be altered in relation to its surroundings, and would therefore appear to be walking *beneath* or *above* the modern floor level, or walking *through* a bricked-in doorway.

All these variants of phenomena have been observed from time to time, and as far as I know no explanation has yet been put forward more convincing than the one I am propounding.

I suggest that this or something similar may be the explanation for the extraordinary spectres which appear without heads, or occasionally with half a torso, or just a hand or pair of legs. The amount of image seen may also be affected by the amount of transmitter which remains intact. If, say, the transmitter were a wall, and the top half of the wall were removed or rebuilt while the lower half remained in position, the likelihood is that only the old lower half would transmit what was registered upon it, the upper half having no imprint or information to transmit. In that event, if the image were of a human figure, only the lower half of that figure would be seen, the imprint of the upper half having been removed with the top of the wall.

Far-fetched? I don't think so. It seems to me that if you accept the basic theory that material surroundings – or more exactly, a *part* of the material surroundings – acts as register (or receiver) and broadcaster (or transmitter), then the rest follows logically.

If you do not accept the theory then you must either disbelieve in these manifestations entirely – and ignore a great deal of evidence – or find an alternative explanation which will serve as well.

So much for the general. Now back to the particular.

Cambridgeshire has less than its share of haunted public-houses, but one or two stand out in reputation. An interesting one is in the west of the county on the A45 from Cambridge to St Neots, and is known as The Caxton Gibbet, being named for its proximity to an old gallows. The gibbet itself still stands, cold and isolated, by the crossroads, about fifty yards below the pub.

The first inn on this site dates back to the eighteenth century, and was no doubt built to accommodate the public thirst generated by each hanging. It was useful, also, to accommodate the corpses. When they were removed from their windy perch, they were laid out on the floor of a room in the inn.

In between executions doubtless the place did good business, as it was on a main highway.

The origin of this story dates back to the hostelry's early days. The landlord was a rogue, and not above using violence to increase his income. On a certain night three wealthy travellers came to the place for a night's lodging. The innkeeper saw what seemed to him easy money and decided to rob the wayfarers during the night.

He was in the act of rifling their baggage and clothing when one of the men awoke. The landlord, in a moment of impulse or panic, killed the man. He was then obliged to kill the other two in order to secure his own safety.

He needed a quick and easy method of getting rid of the bodies, and one was to hand – the well from which the inn's water supply was drawn. All three corpses were disposed of in this way. One assumes the inn found other sources

Left: *Caxton Gibbett*; right: *The Spread Eagle, Croxton*

of water for its needs.

The haunting of the inn is reputed to stem from this multiple murder. Footsteps have been heard walking from the door of the room in which the men were killed; they proceed along the balcony down the staircase and end at the foot of the stairs which is the site of the old well.

In fact, the well still exists, covered by a trapdoor which the present landlord tried in vain to raise for me when I visited the pub.

Manifestations in recent years seem to have been particularly lively during the occupation of the previous landlord and his wife, a Mr and Mrs Clark. The wife had heard the footsteps on many occasions, and her son, Keith, who slept in the room reputed to be the scene of the murder, complained that the temperature in his room was always several degrees lower than that in the rest of the hotel. He had, however, never heard footsteps or any other disturbing sounds.

At the time of my visit, the present landlord had been in occupation only a short time. Although both he and his wife are interested in the pub's history, neither has found any evidence of its being haunted – yet.

I walked down the road a few yards and stood beneath the old gibbet. It was smaller than I had imagined – just high enough on its little knoll to lift a man clear of the ground. The wood was weathered, grey, and there were still the grooves in the crosspiece where the rope had run. Grisly thing. I stood beside it for some minutes, and the atmosphere was stronger there than ever it was in the inn – thick, concentrated and wretchedly miserable. Such a weight of grief and, surprisingly, guilt, there seemed to be beneath that tree. I was not consciously reaching back into time, but the past was growing around me with every minute I stood there.

It was a lorry-driver and his mate who dispelled it. They shot past on the main road, yelling some jocular remark which I failed to catch. No doubt it referred to my inspection of the old gallows. A hundred and fifty years ago travellers on that road took the gibbet less lightly.

Down the A45 towards the Huntingdonshire border stands a second inn, The Spread Eagle. Tradition says that this was the burial ground of those hanged at Caxton. The Spread Eagle is situated at Croxton, but the village is near enough to the crossroads to make the story plausible.

This pub has had its own hauntings. Former licensees, Mr and Mrs Arthur Howe, had heard sounds during the night, as though the bars were crowded. The noises were of people walking about, of banging and similar sounds. The landlord had also heard someone breathing heavily – a particularly nasty noise to hear when there is no sign of the breather!

Again there had been a change of tenancy a few months before I visited the place. The landlady knew of the stories but was closing her mind to them. During her short occupation she had heard nothing unearthly at all and undoubtedly hoped this state of affairs would continue.

All these gibbet tales were a little oppressive, and I was glad to get back to the organised bustle of The Green Man at Trumpington where I was staying. This, too, is an ancient inn, run by a couple of friendly ex-show-business people, Mr and Mrs Charles Shadwell. The name recalled youthful days of listening to a BBC orchestra broadcasting from a series of different studios – and waiting for the inimitable Shadwell laugh.

*The Green Man, Trumpington*

The inn is old enough to house a legion of ghosts, but I could find no trace of any authentic story. Apparently an airman staying in the place had once seen a mysterious lady in his room. No one had given much credence to the tale and it was publicly attributed to a bit of wishful thinking on the part of the room's occupant. He'd had his leg pulled enough to keep him silent on subsequent manifestations, if there were any.

I gave up The Green Man as a bad job from the ghost viewpoint and looked elsewhere. I found what I sought in Madingley.

One of the loveliest houses in eastern England is surely Madingley Hall, a Tudor mansion set among woods and miniature hills. Unlike so many of its period, it has not been allowed to fall into disrepair, or yet been turned over to the National Trust for an empty and echoing monument. Madingley is owned by the University of Cambridge and in term-time is used to accommodate post-graduates; during the vacations the building is used for residential courses. It is a lucky student who finds himself confined to Madingley for two or three weeks.

The place is therefore alive and active as it was in the days when John Hynde built it, *circa* 1543.

If the outside is fascinating, the inside is no less so, for the house is furnished in period and much of the interior fitting is original. There is some fine panelling and moulding and several magnificent tapestries.

*Madingley Hall*

History and legend were interwoven throughout the building. In the attics, approached by an ancient newel stair in the south-east turret, are two murals executed apparently by a local hand in Stuart times. The drawing is rustic in the extreme, but there is a quality of life and energy in the work which convinces of its historical accuracy. The paintings depict bear baiting, boar hunting and falconry, all sports which were practised at Madingley in the seventeenth century. The second attic contains an item of significance, to which I shall return shortly – a fourteenth-century hammer-beam roof.

Two interesting rooms exist on the next floor down – the King's Room and, immediately below it, a small room known as the Dog Hole. According to legend, Charles I hid here after escaping from Childerley Manor, and was betrayed to his pursuers by a barking dog. There seems to be no historical evidence for the story. The King's Room, incidentally, is named not after the luckless Charles, but for Edward VII, who occupied it when Prince of Wales.

There is a great deal more at Madingley than the little I have described; for instance I was shown a large panel, flush with the rest of the panelling in one great room – flush, that is, except for two hinges on the left hand side. The panel was a concealed door; but to what room, passage or stairway? The house is full of unanswered questions, of miniature mysteries. One would need months to investigate them all.

The ghost? She is said to be Lady Ursula Hynde, wife of Sir John, the builder of Madingley, and mother of Sir Francis Hynde. After his father's death, Francis continued with the building of his noble house, and according to an account by Archbishop Laud 'did pull down the Church of St Ethelreda in Histon and the old timbers, lead, bells, and other materials were sold away by him, or employed in the building of his house at Madingley'. It was Francis who took the hammer-beam roof from the consecrated building of either Anglesey Abbey or St Etheldreda's, Histon, and incorporated it into his turret attic. The sacrilege was too much for his mother's piety and old Lady Ursula is said to this day to walk Madingley and its grounds, wringing her hands in grief at her son's unhallowed act.

Who, if anyone, has seen the Lady Ursula?

An au pair girl saw her in 1951. The then Warden of the Hall, Canon Raven, had his grandchildren staying in the house, and the Finnish girl had accompanied them as nursemaid and companion. The girl, who slept in a small bedroom in a turret, was startled one night to be awakened by a little old lady who entered her room. Later the same night, the apparition made a second visit to the room. The girl had known nothing about the ghost prior to this occurrence.

The place is now used as a store room and seems totally without any atmosphere which would suggest haunting.

In fact, the ghost's usual habitat is the path between the hall and the church, where she is said to walk each Christmas Eve, wringing her hands in distress.

During the war a soldier swore to having seen a woman walk across the courtyard at a time when such an occurrence would not have been possible. I have no detailed description of what he saw, although he himself was apparently convinced that it was not flesh and blood. Was it Lady Ursula?

Maybe, but the Lady Ursula Hynde is reputedly not alone in haunting Madingley.

In 1963, a Cambridge woman who was accustomed to walking her dog in the grounds of Madingley Hall called there one day when the grounds were closed to the public. As she approached the hall she heard unmistakable sounds of human voices, and noticed particularly that of a woman – a deep laughing voice. She decided that she had intruded on a garden party, but a little later she had reason to revise that conclusion. At the top of the garden, near the house, she saw a young man sprawling over a stone balustrade. Whether he appeared to her to be dead or not is uncertain. She apparently thought his face resembled a death's head and to be contorted by hate as he looked at her. She noticed that he was wearing a ruff and had his hair cut jaggedly across his forehead. Both the costume detail and the hairstyle suggest the sixteenth century, when the ruff was at the height of its popularity and male hairstyles, though trimmed to show a high forehead, were yet combed forward unevenly at the front.

The Cambridge visitor must have stumbled on the re-creation of an occasion in the time of the hall's first owner and it seems to be the Elizabethan period which is strongest in the house. There are no stories so far as I know of any Madingley hauntings connected with a later period in history than this.

Before being shown the house itself, I had talked to a few local people in the village. Two elderly retired men had been associated with the place for several years in a working capacity, but both said they knew nothing of ghosts there. However, the older of the two knew of the existence of secret passages, for on one occasion many years ago when renovations had been in progress the workman had discovered one such passage. This same man had been lowered into the aperture on a rope in an attempt to trace the route, but when a depth of eighty feet was reached with no sign of a floor to the passageway, he was hauled up again. He thought there had once been steps down from the entrance, but these appeared to have crumbled away.

A short journey across country from Madingley lies Great Wilbraham, an ordinary enough fenland village, pleasant and open and awash with sunshine the day I visited it. It possesses yet another of the many haunted inns.

The Carpenters' Arms is a seventeenth-century house, low-beamed, ceilings a-sag, scheduled as an ancient monument. The haunting is another footsteps manifestation and the experiences seem to have been in the realm of sound only. No one has actually *seen* anything here.

The present licensee, Mrs Paula Grosvenor-Brown, has regularly heard footsteps proceeding along an upstairs corridor. The steps always cease at the same place. She has also heard the handle of her bedroom door rattling as it is turned.

Once during her husband's lifetime, she heard the footsteps – not then so familiar and recognisable as they are now – and asked him if some of the pub's visitors had returned as she could hear people walking about. He replied that they had not and that the upstairs premises were empty.

An employee, Mrs Joyce Carroll, was downstairs one day preparing a meal for two residents. She had not begun to cook the food when she heard the sounds of footsteps walking along the upstairs corridor. She assumed the obvious, being rather disconcerted that the guests had returned before the meal was ready for them. On investigation, of course, it was found that the walker was not one of the guests and the upstairs premises were unoccupied.

On yet another occasion a regular visitor to the pub heard a knock at one of the doors, and this was also heard by Mrs Grosvenor-Brown. Inevitably, no person had knocked.

This particular haunting is of long standing, for a family who kept the pub sixty years ago had also heard the sounds. Several members of this family (named Barber) had heard the steps, and all were agreed that they always stopped at the same place.

The origin of the haunting seems to be unknown, as is the name of the haunter. Easy to be blasé and dismiss this as another example of the ghost known by its footsteps alone. Less easy to live with these unexplained, unnerving noises year after year. Irritating, too, in a way, not to be able either to *know* what is at the bottom of it or to influence its behaviour-pattern.

There seems no doubt that more people hear ghosts than see them, and those who do both are rare. People either 'receive' in one way or the other; hardly ever is the manifestation both audible and visible to the one person. Therefore even though three persons experience a haunting, it is quite possible for two of the subjects to hear but not see the ghost and the third to see but not hear. An interesting state of affairs.

One type of experience which combines audio with visual demonstration – though of the effects rather than the actual presence of a ghost – is that of the poltergeist. So far in this book little has been said of this type of phenomenon, largely because it is less common than the 'repeated incident' or 'pattern' type of haunting.

However, an occurrence of this nature was reported at Gorefield in the Isle of Ely in February 1923.

The people concerned were fruit farmers by the name of Scrimshaw and were a family of three, Joseph Scrimshaw, his elderly mother, and his fifteen-year-old daughter, Olive. They lived a quiet life until the night of 14 February, the festival of St Valentine.

Olive and her grandmother shared a bedroom in the small house in which they lived and it was the girl who was awakened by a noise on the landing outside the bedroom door. She woke her grandmother, who, on opening the door, found that a wicker stand had fallen. This was only the beginning of a series of violent events which continued throughout the night. Washstands were hurled across beds, mirrors torn out of their frames and furniture moved about. At one point all the china on every shelf in the pantry fell from the shelves and smashed.

The most dramatic event of a traumatic night must have been the moment when an Angelus Pianola, said to weigh five hundredweight, slid from its place against the wall, hurtled round the room and finally fell with a mighty crash. Five days later the extraordinary business was repeated, somewhat less violently. The local vicar was called in and expressed the opinion that the disturbances might be due to natural physical causes – in this case the fact that a dyke near the house had been dug out deeply the previous year, and at the time of the haunting carried an excessive amount of water. However, undermining by water seemed an unlikely reason to the house's inhabitants. A local exorcist was summoned, and although her routine seems, by any standards, to have been a bit unusual – hair, nail parings and apple seeds, burned together – the haunting ceased.

But the Scrimshaws were not yet free of their tormentor. On 17 March, Mrs Holmes, the exorcist, died suddenly. Two days later the poltergeist returned to the Scrimshaw's farm. Ornaments fell from the bedroom mantelpiece, a three-gallon earthenware water filter crashed to the floor and a pitcher on a nearby table also smashed. That apparently was the end of the matter, no more was heard of the demonstrator and no further disturbances occurred.

You will see how different this type of manifestation is from the ordinary haunting. There is no pattern apart from that of violence and no apparent human association connecting events of the present with those in the past.

However, within their particular group all poltergeist hauntings are similar. There is always a great deal of noise, much smashing of china and violent displacement of furniture and other objects. Most significant of all is the fact that invariably the manifestations occur in a household which contains an adolescent child. Indeed from time to time, the adolescents in afflicted houses are accused of being actually responsible for the disturbances.

In most cases any direct responsibility, in the sense that the child actually throws or breaks articles, can be discounted. What cannot be disregarded is that the adolescent may be indirectly and involuntarily the cause of the manifestation.

Poltergeist hauntings are above all demonstrations of violent energy. All hauntings require the use of some energy – and here I use the word in the sense of power rather than activity – but to produce poltergeist symptoms requires the kind of animal and physical force which is present in high degree in puberty.

*How* this force is used, and by whom or what, is a debatable question. Is it a force-field, of the same kind as a magnetic field? Has the dormant energy of the child an explosive property which some incident or condition is able to trigger into apparently detached physical demonstration?

One thing is certain; that this is not the kind of manifestation which may be left behind by a change of material surroundings. Poltergeist demonstrations can follow their victims from one place to another. Since, when a family moves, the children move also, the conclusion must be drawn that the haunting is associated with person rather than place.

Another feature of this type of haunting is that the symptoms usually last for a limited time only – as though after a while the energy supply ceased to be powerful enough to generate violent activity.

My own feeling is that manifestations of this nature are not caused by malevolent or mischievous spirits, but by a kind of self-generated natural force which expresses itself in physical terms much in the way that lightning does.

A story which has certain features in common with poltergeist disturbance yet is different enough to make me hesitate to describe it as such was told me by Mrs Cynthia Rule, who lives now in Essex, but who for the first seven years of her marriage lived in Mill Lane, Ickleton, Cambridgeshire.

The Rules occupied one of a pair of semi-detached cottages, built some time in the eighteenth century near the site of an old fulling-mill. The mill itself has long been pulled down, but it is possible that at one time both cottages had housed its employees.

The two children of the family were born within fifteen months of each other, but nothing untoward occurred in the cottage until after the birth of the second child, a son.

One night, after the parents had retired to bed they were alarmed to hear an extraordinary noise in their bedroom. 'It sounded,' said Mrs Rule, 'exactly like a small motor-bike.' Unable to identify the source of the sound, they got up to investigate. Eventually the din was traced to a small cupboard under a flight of stairs leading to the attic; the stairs came through the Rules' bedroom.

There seemed no cause for the noise, but Mrs Rule removed some shoes which were the only objects in the cupboard. The noise persisted, however, and by now thoroughly unnerved, Cynthia Rule went downstairs to make a cup of tea. When she returned to bed the sound had ceased.

Her husband was convinced that there must be a rational explanation for the phenomenon, and by the next morning both of them were inclined to make light of their experience.

The next night exactly the same thing occurred. Again they investigated and again could find no cause for the sound they heard.

To use Mrs Rule's words, 'It wouldn't be true to say this happened every night, but it lasted for six months and didn't miss many nights. When it finally stopped we couldn't believe it and would lie awake waiting for it to start again, which, thank goodness, it never did in *our* house.'

In matters of this kind there is a reluctance on the part of the sufferers to discuss the matter outside the family, or even to mention it to near relatives for fear of ridicule. The Rules had not even told their next door neighbour of the peculiarity and it was not until they had left the house that they heard the next instalment of the story.

About a year after the above happenings, their former neighbour, Mrs Morris, told Cynthia Rule how worried she and her family were about an unusual noise which began every night in their son's bedroom. The disturbance was always preceded by three loud knocks, followed by the noise of a motor-cycle. It was so loud that the boy could not sleep and was very frightened. This experience was even odder than that of the Rules, for the sound was coming from a solid brick outside wall. The noise continued intermittently for six months then was never heard again.

In her letter to me Mrs Rule said that both cottages had recently been renovated and were up for sale. It will be interesting to see if the new occupants suffer any disturbance.

Theories? Well, whatever it was, the sound is unlikely to have been that of a motor-cycle. Had it been outside the cottage there would have been a possibility, but no one keeps motor-cycles in bedrooms – at least not in cottage bedrooms.

A poltergeist? The three knocks are likely enough, and there is the common factor of a child-association present, but there is no hint of any violence, no characteristic throwing around of furniture or smashing of china. What we have is a whirring or humming noise, the type of sound made by a piece of machinery.

I suggest that what the Rules and the Morrises heard was the sound of an old spinning-wheel.

In the eighteenth century the wool industry was largely a cottage one; certainly the spinning process was carried out in the cottages, usually by women and children. The men were the weavers, and this process normally took place in a larger building – a forerunner of the modern factory.

The child labour used was often that of quite young children – five or six years old – and it could well have been that these cottages had been the scene of wool-spinning activities with the children of the family employed. The proximity of the fulling-mill is an indication of the kind of industry present locally. The fact that in both the cases of haunting young children were present in the house is significant.

Perhaps it was the presence of children and their particular kind of energy which triggered off the haunting in each case. I cannot see how this works, but it seems to me that if the child-spinner theory is correct, the presence of children at a later stage in time in the same surroundings might generate whatever was necessary to reproduce the original scene. There are similarities here to the haunting at Brooke in Norfolk, where the old schoolteacher appeared only to those who were childless – a haunting with pre-selected conditions.

I find this a most intriguing story, and have a feeling that I shall hear more of it.

I had a tale of the archetypal kind from a fellow-writer resident in Cambridge, whom I will call Clare Duval,* though only the initials accord with her own name.

One evening Mrs Duval and her husband were driving along Arbury Road on the fringes of Cambridge. The time of year was midsummer, and darkness still lay an hour or two ahead. It was apparently a pleasant evening and neither occupant of the car was prepared for what happened. Without warning, a huge black, wolf-like animal appeared and leapt over the bonnet of the car. The Duval's car was of the vintage type with a long bonnet, and to leap across it needed considerable power and agility. The animal vanished into an allotment on the far side of the road, and although the couple at once left their car and searched the area no trace of the creature was found. What the Duvals did notice, however, was a sensation of extreme cold, in spite of the summer weather, and the abject terror of their own dog, which they had left in the back of the car.

A significant factor in this occurrence is that Arbury is the site of an Iron Age Settlement, the inhabitants of which no doubt had an adequate share of superstitious fear, religious practice and objects either of fetish or racial memory.

I am disposed to think that the black dog (for this is our old acquaintance Black Shuck or the padfoot) is an archetypal memory of the earliest known horse. A possible alternative explanation is that it represents a wolf, perhaps used as a fetish-symbol by our remote ancestors and the image passed down via human genes as a memory (deep-buried, perhaps but not totally lost) of the days when wolves were feared and then placated by worship or magic. Racial memory is a deep, rich and largely untapped store of knowledge – and tells as much about the history of Man's development as it does about his early beliefs. Unfortunately this knowledge is largely lost to us because of our disregard of its existence.

The padfoot traditionally is a harbinger of ill-luck, and it proved so in this case, for within days of his appearance the Duvals suffered an irreparable financial loss. Shortly afterwards Clare Duval's husband developed the kidney disease which was to prove fatal.

One wonders what awesome rites in ancient times associated this creature with disaster. Was it, like the flowering May, once linked with human sacrifice? There is not enough information available to be sure that the guess is accurate.

From a premonitory ghost with its overtones of dread, I was glad to turn to a brighter landscape and visit one of the loveliest Elizabethan houses in England.

Sawston Hall is pure Tudor, unalloyed and unmodified, and has been the property of the Huddleston family since the sixteenth century. Earlier still it belonged to John Neville, brother of Warwick the Kingmaker, though the echoes which it holds are of Tudor not Plantagenet times.

Much has been written of this beautiful building – too much, perhaps, for I think the present owners must have grown very weary of the constant talk and investigation of ghosts in connection with their home.

Ghosts or not, I fell hopelessly in love with the old house. I would like to have stayed in it, lived in it, swept up and down the stairs with skirts flowing and farthingale brushing the banisters. Empty and echoing though it is now, its atmosphere is compelling.

The hall is now owned by Major Eyre, nephew of the previous owner, the late Captain Reginald Eyre-Huddleston. Mrs Clare Huddleston, the captain's widow, has had her own experiences of Sawston's ghosts. On many occasions she heard the sound of a spinet being played, though no such instrument was in the house.

At a later date similar music was heard by a guest staying at the hall, and once again there was no rational explanation for the sound. Spinet music is delicious – light and delicate as lace – and one can imagine the embroidery of it across the air of the great rooms on spring evenings. Mrs Huddleston never feared this ghostly echo.

An echo of a different kind reached Major Eyre when, some years ago he was helping to open the house to the public. A number of young girls had been engaged to act as guides, and while he was waiting in the downstairs hall for them to arrive he heard a peal of female laughter from the upper rooms. His first thought was that the girls had already come in by another entrance and were now upstairs. However, when he searched, the house was empty. The guides arrived some time later. The laughter he had heard was not of here and now.

*Sawston Hall*

As I stood in the great hall where Major Eyre himself had waited, I felt a sensation of great happiness and joy – almost, I was about to write, of comfort. There are parts of Sawston which do not have this warmth, but the hall most surely is an area which has known human happiness and gaiety.

Sawston's history, however, is as varied as that of the Huddlestons themselves. In July 1553, following the death of the boy Edward VI, an attempt was made by John Dudley, Duke of Northumberland, to place Lady Jane Grey on the throne of England. Jane Grey was cousin to Edward VI and to Mary, his sister, the rightful heir to the throne, but it was in Northumberland's interests to see Jane, rather than Mary, queen.

John Dudley planned a strategem, intending to lure both Mary and her younger sister, Elizabeth, to London by news of the young king's illness. Once he had the girls in the capital it would have been a simple matter to capture and imprison them. What their fate would have been afterwards is open to speculation. It is fairly certain they would have had short lives.

Mary had set out from Hertfordshire post-haste on hearing that her brother was on his death-bed. (Elizabeth, who was cannier, gave out that she herself was too ill to travel.) The elder sister had reached Hoddesdon when she had warning that Northumberland had sent his son, Robert Dudley, to intercept her and ensure her safe arrival into the jaws of the waiting trap.

The princess and her escort at once turned their horses and began to ride towards Norfolk and safety. It was late in the day, however, and Mary was weary. One of her escort, Andrew Huddleston, suggested that they might rest the night at his family home at Sawston. The Huddlestons had always been a staunchly Catholic family, and this seemed a good suggestion.

So Mary Tudor and her small group of attendants descended on the Huddlestons at Sawston and the princess slept in the four-poster bed, which still stands in the same bedroom today. She had been asleep only a short time when a message was brought that Robert Dudley and his force were approaching Sawston bent on the capture of their quarry. The princess's host, John Huddleston, woke her immediately and, according to tradition, Mary escaped dressed as a milkmaid, riding behind a manservant of the house.

A charming story, whether or not the escape trimmings are true. What is true apparently is that the fugitives looked back at one point and saw a great building blazing furiously behind them. Robert Dudley had reached Sawston Hall.

Afterwards when Mary Tudor was Queen of England, when Jane Grey and Dudley of Northumberland were both beheaded, John Huddleston rebuilt Sawston, and was knighted by his grateful sovereign. The Huddlestons have always been true to their religion, no matter what the price of that loyalty.

In Elizabeth's reign that price began to rise. To practise a different religion from the one currently in power was to court danger and since the Huddlestons refused to deviate from their beliefs, they must have lived constantly on guard and under strain. In order to safeguard the travelling priests who celebrated mass whenever they could for the Catholic families, Sawston provided three priest's holes. Only one is to be seen now, and I was informed by workers at the hall that the other two are fallen into disrepair – or perhaps their location is not known.

The remaining secret room is almost impossible to find without foreknowledge. It is built into the thickness of the tower wall and is reached by a trapdoor in the floor of a dark landing. It is just big enough for a man to stand or lie in and claustrophobic in the extreme. However, this would be of no account when your life depended on staying hidden until the searchers had departed.

Some ten or twelve years ago investigations into the Sawston ghosts were carried out by Tom Corbett, a clairvoyant, and Diana Norman, a journalist. They stayed the night at Sawston and although Mrs Norman's room was thought to be haunted, she slept undisturbed. The clairvoyant, who was sleeping in the Tapestry Room which had been Mary Tudor's, and in the four-poster which the Queen had occupied four hundred years earlier, was not allowed the sleep of the just. From 4.00 a.m. onwards Tom Corbett was awakened every hour on the hour.

He had set his alarm clock for 7.00 a.m., but at four o'clock it shrilled in his ear. He awoke to hear the handle of his door being rattled. At five the alarm clock sang out again, although the alarm hand still pointed to seven. He heard someone prowling around the Panelled Room nearby. At six the clock again sounded the alarm and again Corbett thought his room was being checked.

Now what type of individual would check a place with that degree of regularity? Corbett's answer was a night watchman. He thought, also, that the man had a name like 'Cutless' or something similar. Later Mrs Huddleston discovered that a family in the village bore the name of 'Cutriss'. Was the watchman an ancestor? It is possible.

Prior to the Corbett-Norman investigation, the Tapestry Room was supposed to be haunted by a Lady in Grey. I had heard (inevitably) that Mary Tudor herself was the spectre.

Many times knocks and sounds have been heard coming from the Panelled Room, and several guests at various times have been disturbed by knocks and rattlings at their bedroom doors.

I talked to two employees of the hall, Miss Eva Plogz and Mrs Mozley. The great house is empty of furniture since the death of Captain Huddleston, and Miss Plogz lives alone there, as a housekeeper-caretaker. She told me that she always feels 'a sense of presence' – note the singular rather than the plural here – but is not at all afraid in the building.

She also had an interesting story of the time when Sawston Hall became the scene of a Marlon Brando film, and of a curious occurrence in connection with it.

The film was *The Nightcomers*, the latest version of Henry James's mysterious story, *The Turn of the Screw*. The film makers found Sawston an ideal setting for that strange tale of the haunted children and the adults involved with them.

Two security officials were employed by the film company, and one imagines there can have been little for them to do. Villagers were used as extras in the film and for the rest there was the film company with its stars, administrators, technicians. So the two men must have had ample time to wander round the hall and take in its atmosphere.

As far as I know they saw nothing untoward, but on one occasion they heard music coming from the chapel. On investigation the building was found to be empty and silent, but the men were not to be moved from their story. Music had been playing in the chapel, played by whom and for what purpose, no one could say. Not this time Mrs Huddleston's spinet, I think, but possibly a re-creation of a Mass said long since for the benefit of Huddlestons centuries dead and gone.

Mrs Mozley had her own story to tell. On one occasion it was part of her duties to arrange the flowers for a forthcoming function in the hall, and she was working in the Long Gallery of the house. Her husband was also in the building, and had said that he would shortly join her. She was walking along the Gallery when she felt a hand laid on her shoulder. Thinking it to be her husband, she turned to speak to him, only to find herself alone. She assured me there was no doubt that *someone* or *something* had touched her on the shoulder.

For myself, on going through the hall I saw nothing save the fine rooms, the panelling, the moulded ceilings. Only in the Tapestry Room I felt the familiar chill of cold air; and in the Great Hall the warmth of a lost and distant happiness. If Madingley has the feeling of a living present, Sawston has the feeling of a living past. The house stands now, lovely, untenanted, waiting, looking out on a landscape which can have changed little in the last four hundred years. The ghosts carry on their lives as they always have, not heeding the passing of Time.

A story with a different atmosphere is that of Mr D. G. Morris* of Arlington. Before the events took place which I am about to relate, Mr Morris was totally sceptical on the subject of the supernatural, believing that such stories were the products of over-imaginative minds. He is no longer a sceptic and judging by the experiences of his family at No. 2 Croydon Road, Arlington, this is not surprising.

At the time of the occurrences, the Morris family were living in the council house at Croydon Road which Mr Morris describes as rather a poor place to live in, 'no bathroom, no hot water, no flush toilet'. Life had been hard for the family for some time. The group of five council houses was situated on a lonely stretch of road and the Morrises had no form of transport to ease the isolation. Douglas Morris himself was working in a poorly paid job, and altogether the family lived a frugal and somewhat depressed existence.

As a result of the situation the head of the household was feeling in low enough spirits one day to be caught by an advertisement for the opening of Joanna Southcott's Box.

Now, although I know nothing of this box, its history or its contents, I do know that advertisements regarding its opening have been current in the national press for a good thirty years and possibly longer. I will quote here from Mr Morris's letter.

This was some sort of religious movement originated by, I believe a Catholic organisation at Bedford. I cut out the coupon and sent it off and some days later received a number of religious literature pamphlets. I wrote back and said that I was suffering from a feeling of despair and misery due to financial difficulties and asked for help. In return I received a piece of white linen approx. 2″ square and given instructions which are a little hazy now, but [sic] involved putting this linen into a bottle of water and using small amounts of water from the bottle each day in washing hands, washing up dishes, in bath water etc, and making a wish at the same time in great concentration. Well, no benefits appeared to materialise and I thought nothing further about this and in fact did not at the time connect it with future events (if indeed they were connected).

Some time after this event a series of small incidents occurred in the household. A medicine cabinet on the kitchen wall which had a front mirror began to slip from its position. At one moment, Mr Morris would be using it to shave in, then as soon as he turned away the whole cabinet would move askew. He would straighten it, only to find shortly afterwards that it had again shifted. The strange thing about this happening was that whenever the Morrises *tried* to make the cabinet hang crooked they could not do so. It fell back into its normal straight position.

The next thing they noticed was that the key to the back door would neither lock nor unlock the door and eventually a new lock had to be fixed. A further and perhaps more significant event was that the key to the coalhouse door disappeared and the door could no longer be locked.

The coalhouse was part of the main house, but only accessible from the outside, and it was from this part of the house that the Morrises began to hear noises at night. Several times Douglas Morris rushed downstairs and outside to the coalhouse door with a torch, to see who was inside the place. But the door was always found shut, and the coalhouse empty.

During these manifestations, Mrs Morris also was experiencing odd phenomena but neither she nor her husband mentioned the occurrences for fear of ridicule. The son of the house, a young boy at the time, slept in a small bedroom immediately over the coalhouse and he was undergoing a frightening series of events. The child was so afraid that he slept with the bedclothes pulled over his head and even so on several occasions he felt something drop on to the bed when in fact nothing of the kind had occurred. He also consistently heard noises from the coalhouse below. He mentioned the matter to his mother, but at this stage she thought he must be dreaming and did not take the account seriously.

One afternoon Mr Morris returned home to find the house empty. His wife had left a note to say that she had taken the children to her mother's for the afternoon and had left his lunch prepared. He ate the meal and was about to settle down in an armchair, when he heard a sound which in the circumstances he knew to be an impossibility – the sound of footsteps walking across the floor of one of the empty bedrooms. After a blood-freezing moment, he went upstairs to investigate. He looked inside two of the bedrooms and found them empty, then he went to his son's room, but before he could enter it, the door handle 'suddenly started rattling like mad – a very loud persistent rattle as if someone was inside and trying frantically to get out'.

While the man stood petrified, gazing at the door handle, he felt a sudden blast of air *from the closed door*, and a damp shapeless mass of what seemed to be grey mist rushed at him. Understandably Mr Morris was absolutely rooted with fear. As he says himself, 'the fear of the unknown and the knowledge suddenly that there were some things outside of human existence'. He flew down the stairs in terror and slammed the door of the living-room behind him. After that he heard no more sounds. When his wife returned he did not mention the matter, probably by this time being occupied with explaining the occurrence rationally to himself.

Later his wife escorted their son to bed. No one had been upstairs since the time of Mr Morris's experience until that moment. There was no knowing what they would find in the bedroom. However, his wife came down and said nothing, and he assumed that nothing untoward had happened. He still did not mention his own experience and it was not until some weeks later that the matter was brought into the open.

From this point I will quote from Mr Morris's own graphic letter.

Some weeks later one evening after all the family except my wife and I were in bed we were sitting in the living-room when I heard footsteps coming from upstairs again. This time, my wife and I were together for the first time, when this happened, and of course, we couldn't ignore it. We looked at each other and my wife said 'do you hear those footsteps,' I said 'Yes,' and although we knew that nobody ever got out of bed and walked about, I said I would go up and investigate. While the footsteps could still be heard I went upstairs and although only a matter of seconds had elapsed while I got upstairs, everyone was fast asleep in their bed, and the bedclothes were undisturbed. No one had got up.

When I went downstairs and told my wife, she then revealed what she had been experiencing, and I did the same. This was the first time we both realised that the same things had been happening to us both. Now that we did not fear being laughed at we were able to tell each other all the things that had happened. I then heard about the happenings in my stepson's bedroom (things falling on the bed) about the noises and footsteps and most important – the 'thing' in our son's bedroom. My wife told me that the night she returned from her mother's and took the boy up to bed, as she opened the door, this grey shapeless mass and rush of air had come out at them and the boy just flew into her arms. She did not scream or make a fuss so as not to frighten the boy still further and also because this had happened to her before. On one occasion she had experienced the door handle rattling when she was INSIDE the room on her own. She says she never knew how she managed to get out she was so terrified and almost struck paralysed.

At a later period, the family even fastened down the windows in all the bedrooms in case a cat was responsible for the disturbances, though they had little faith in this explanation. Matters were no better, and they still heard noises and footsteps in the house.

Finally, when both parents were reduced to a low state of health and spirits by the manifestations, they managed to find another home and escape from the much-pestered No. 2.

Another family resides in the building now, but no one has heard a complaint from them – perhaps because extensive modernisation has taken place to the haunted area of the house.

What is the explanation for this extraordinary series of occurrences? Mr Morris is convinced that whatever occupied the house was evil. He makes various conjectures regarding the influence of the linen from the Joanna Southcott's Box people (though personally I think the commencement of the pestering was coincidental with the supply of the linen). He also raises the question of the occasional mysterious bands of fog which bedevil the M1 and which have been responsible for atrocious accidents.

Looking back over stories encountered earlier, one can trace certain interesting similarities to the Morrises' tale, and Mr Morris's theory. The band of mist, for instance, which lies over the Cawthorpe plantation road at the haunted spot; the enveloping fog which concealed the Boadicea emanation; and – a story which I have not yet narrated – the laughing mist at Borley in Essex. It seems that what we term mist or fog can be one of the symptoms of supernatural manifestation.

The subject of this story is convinced that what he and his family experienced was an evil spirit, and he states, 'There is nothing humorous about ghosts – nor anything logical.' Individual spirit, evil or otherwise? Or recorded transmission of long-past events and emotions? Each theory has its supporters.

One other strange thing about No. 2 Croydon Road. Some of the Morrises' predecessors in the house are said to have been a strange couple who spoke to no one. It seems that during their occupation the wife disappeared from the house, but the village minded its own business and no one made enquiries as to her whereabouts.

Finally a story of a modern ghost. A friend of mine in the BBC, Michael Chapman, produced an early-morning radio programme which went out to the East Anglian region. When he knew that I was writing this book, he told me of an experience of his own in the county of Cambridge.

Michael comes from the northern half of the county – the area known for centuries as the Isle of Ely, named no doubt in the days when the environs of Ely town really were an island in the fen water.

On this particular day, the Chapman family had been on a day trip to Southend and were returning very late at night on the coach which had been engaged to transport the whole party of holidaymakers. Michael was then a young child of about five, but remembers the day's events with particular clarity because he had distinguished himself by getting lost that morning on Southend pier.

The coach had passed through the village of Milton, when abruptly there was a violent thump on the offside of the vehicle, as though it had struck or been struck by something on the road. At the same time all the lights in the bus were extinguished. The coach was by now at a standstill, and driver and passengers got out to see what had happened.

No doubt they expected to see another vehicle of some kind, and possible serious injuries to its occupants. However, apart from their own coach, the road was found to be completely empty, and there was no apparent cause for the occurrence.

Mystified, passengers and driver climbed back on board, discussing what the incident might mean. It was at this point that someone recollected the story of a ghostly car which was reputed to drive along that stretch of road. No one, it seems, knew the car's history.

There is still a crossroads in this place, though now it marks the turning off to a housing estate. I have heard of no later reports of ghost vehicles being encountered here, though incidents may have occurred. Possibly the ghostly car and its collision with the bus – if this is what the occurrence was – is an echo of an accident in the recent past. Spectral cars, though rarer than phantom coaches, are not unheard of.

Overall, as I said at the beginning of this chapter, Cambridge produced few ghost stories, and its inhabitants showed more reluctance to discuss the subject than in other areas. I was given a likely explanation by a correspondent in the north of the county. She suggested that the strong Puritan indoctrination during the seventeenth century might have led the local people to believe that ghosts were of the devil, and therefore not to be admitted into the realms of possibility. I thought this feasible until I considered the history of Huntingdonshire. Did not the latter give birth to the Lord Protector, Oliver Cromwell? And yet it is rich and fecund in its stories of hauntings. Its people showed neither fear of nor distaste for their ghosts, but accepted these echoes of the past as an integral part of the present. So the reason for Cambridgeshire's relatively unhaunted state remains a mystery.

# HERTFORDSHIRE
## A Grocer, a Searcher and a Homesick American Airman

Hertfordshire is in some respects a baffling county, in that it has no collective feeling or corporate identity. The south of the area is very much a Home County, with the influence of London strong and apparent; the north is true East Anglian in feeling, with strong links to Cambridgeshire and the nearby fen country. The landscape is far from fenland, however, and consists of short rolling hills, good patches of woodland (no doubt surviving from the great Royal forests of historic times), and beautiful secluded hamlets reminiscent of every foreigner's idea of the typical English village. The people of this northern area are warm, friendly, alive and with a splendid richness and variety of character. They like nothing better than to chat to you over the village Post Office counter, or offer you a cup of tea or coffee while you talk and ask questions.

I suspect that the traffic in this part of Hertfordshire is much more east to west than north to south. The dividing line seems to come somewhere between Buntingford and Hatfield, for the former still belongs in the old world while the latter and all points south is emphatically of the new.

This county of interesting contrasts produced an equally interesting, and perhaps predictable pattern of hauntings.

Most of the good stories came from the northern parts and as one moved south, nearer the Metropolis, nearer the twentieth-century whirlpool of traffic, business, affairs of the world, the fewer were those echoes of the past which ghost stories epitomise. One may draw one's own conclusions from this.

I began investigations in Royston, a prosperous market town not far from the Cambridgeshire border. The place stands in an interesting position geographically, being at the junction of two Roman roads, Ermine Street and the Icknield Way. There was almost certainly a Roman military station here during the occupation and both Roman and Saxon traces have been found in the area. Even the Romans were not the first on the scene, for a British settlement was established here before Caesar ever placed his sandalled foot on the south coast sands.

Royston; the name suggests Roy's or Roi's Town, King's Town, but the local people assured me the place was called after a noblewoman who resided in the district, Lady Roysia. Of this lady and her history I have no knowledge, but Royston boasts other and more convincing memorabilia to the powers of the past. James I had a palace here, the remains of which still stand, though the structure fronting the street appears to be of a much later period than the Jacobean. However, the place had its moment in history, for here James Stuart signed Walter Raleigh's death warrant, sending that proud, unlucky courtier to the block to please Spain. Here also the king received the startling and unwelcome news of the Gunpowder Plot.

Apparently Royston Palace registered no unpleasant associations for James, however. He had a hunting-lodge built on the outskirts of the town, and both palace and lodge were in frequent use. No doubt Royston was a convenient stopping-place on progress or for recreation and the nearby forest must have afforded good runnable stags for a hunt-loving king. Some of his hunting habits, like the rest of his social manners, are disgusting to modern taste, but James I was not the most attractive of monarchs or men.

Royston holds other items of historical interest. Saxon tumuli were found outside the town. More mysterious than these is the town's cave – a man-made excavation thought to have been a headquarters of that extraordinary sect, the Knights Templar.

Neither the knights nor the tumuli appeared to offer me what I was seeking, and on first enquiry it seemed that Royston was totally unhaunted. Such was not the case.

I had heard that the Old Priory (whose name describes its origin) had a ghost – reputedly that of a monk. The priory survives mainly in the form of a beautiful Georgian building, divided into three sets of apartments. From enquiries it was apparent that the building is not now haunted, if it ever was. It is a curious fact that wherever a convent, an abbey or priory once stood, there is a local expectation that it must be haunted. Perhaps this is the deep-seated fear of the results of sacrilege so firmly implanted in generations of our Christian forefathers that even in this agnostic century we are unable to shake it off.

From the priory I was directed to another old building in the town – a structure which had until recent times housed a grocery business trading in the name of A. E. Baker and Co., but now occupied by the Oxfam authorities. Oxfam seem unlucky in their choice of premises, for this was the second of their shops I encountered, and both are haunted.

The Royston building is rambling, consisting of a long ground-floor room, now used as a salesroom for the Society's goods and two sets of upstairs premises, that on the right being two small rooms, that on the left being two or three little rooms, once occupied as a flat. Each is connected to the ground floor by a separate staircase, though the first runs straight down into the shop, while the other leads to a door into the backyard of the premises. From the yard a covered passage runs at right angles to the shop, emerging in a nearby street. Here the loading and unloading of groceries took place in former days.

Before approaching the scene of the story I had interviewed two people who were formerly employed by A. E. Baker and Co. The first, Mr Sharp, had been manager there; the second, Mrs Lawrence, had been an employee of the firm for sixteen years. Both their accounts confirmed that there had been a series of inexplicable occurrences in the building over a long period of time.

One of the staff had 'seen something' on the stairs (those leading to the upstairs premises on the right hand side of the shop) and had apparently walked right through it. It was not clear what actually had been seen.

At various times, all members of the staff had heard footsteps in these upstairs rooms when no human was present there.

The manifestations were not confined to noise only. On one occasion a wide shelf containing a variety of goods was completely cleared, the contents being found on the floor. Another time a teapot was found upside down on the floor. On other occasions goods were moved about from their original places, though they had not been touched by either employees or customers.

At one stage an occupant of the flat over the left hand side of the shop heard glasses and bottles being moved in the cellar under the premises. This sound had also been heard by a cleaner and by the shop's area manager.

A frequent manifestation was a sharp drop in temperature having no apparent cause. And the removal and disturbance of goods was constant – all manner of stuff was found moved from its normal place, including items as heavy as tins of biscuits. At one time, a stand containing cider bottles lifted from the floor, causing the bottles to rattle.

Usually the noises were heard during the day, though, since apart from the inhabitant of the flat the premises were only occupied during working hours, there may have been other manifestations after dark.

Only once has there been a sighting. During the flat's occupation by a Mrs Deare, the figure of a man was seen, in a corner of one of the downstairs rooms.

Mr Sharp and Mrs Lawrence said the general opinion of the shop's staff was that the disturbing presence was that of a former owner. Also the manifestations appeared to be worse at certain times of the year, though they could not remember which seasons were most affected.

After this interview I went to the shop itself and was shown round by two of the Oxfam staff on duty. The ladies had heard nothing of any ghost, and were not disposed to worry about it if they did.

'We are on shift duty,' one explained, 'and we are only here for two or three hours at a time. It is unlikely we should notice anything. And anyway we are always too busy.' This last was true; during the short time I was in the place there was a constant stream of customers in and out of the downstairs room.

My guides showed me first the right side upper rooms with the staircase leading into the shop proper. These were the rooms allegedly haunted, and I had been told that the room particularly affected was that nearest the stairs. It was affected all right, there was certainly a feeling of discomfort in the first room. The room beyond, however, was considerably worse and the feeling of unease was so intense that I was glad to leave it. Having met this sensation several times by now, I recognised it and saw no reason to prolong the experience.

We inspected the second set of rooms which had formerly been a flat. This was now in poor repair, but depressing though the rooms were, the sense of oppression was absent from them.

The only other part of the structure with any atmosphere was the covered-in passageway leading to the back street. Here I had the sensation that barrels had been rolled up and down this alley for many years. An easy enough conclusion to come to and I claim no occult significance for it.

One last incident occurred at the end of my visit. In a final conversation, I asked the lady assistants if they had ever noticed that goods were disturbed in the shop.

'Oh yes. But it's usually the people on the shift before us who don't tidy up properly.'

'Are you sure?'

'Well – no. But we always leave things tidy and then when we come on duty again, we sometimes find articles on the floor.'

'Like last week,' chimed in one assistant. 'Everything on this counter was swept into a jumbled heap in the middle.'

'I had thought,' said another, 'that I would have a word with the previous shift, as they really should leave things in a better state.'

'Perhaps before you blame them,' I said, 'you should talk to the people who worked here in the days before Oxfam took over. The activities you describe sound very like those of their ghostly grocer.'

I left a trio of startled workers and went out into the afternoon sunlight.

Incredible as it may sound, a nearby shop on the same side of the High Street is said to be haunted. This is the hairdresser's shop of Mr Arthur Thair, who states that he does not believe in ghosts, but who told me of some strange happenings during his father's occupancy and his own.

One of the clients of Mr Thair, senior, was a member of a well-known banking family and it was he who told the hairdresser that one of the upstairs rooms – known as the Tudor Room – was haunted by a woman. Arthur Thair's eldest sister would never sleep in this particular room.

There was an occasion when Arthur drew a design for another of his sisters which she pinned to her bedroom wall. She awoke one night just in time to see the picture float free of the wall, turn once or twice in the air and land on her bed.

After the death of Arthur Thair's parents, he had the so-called haunted room converted into a ladies' hairdressing salon. When floorboards were taken up in order to wire the room for electricity, a quantity of bones was found, sawn up small and accompanied by a piece of whipcord. Whether the bones were human or animal, whether put there by mortal agency or merely by rats, none will ever know now. Mr Thair, in the interests of a quiet life and a peaceful professional existence, consigned the relics to the dustbin.

Mr Thair himself has had only one strange experience in the haunted room. A year or two ago he was trimming a child's hair when both he and the mother of the child heard someone walk into the room. They turned to see who the newcomer was, only to find the place empty apart from themselves.

These two stories of Royston High Street may be connected but I think it unlikely. In the case of the Oxfam shop, the significant factor is the physical removal of goods from one place to another. Occasionally in these house hauntings one hears of minor movement taking place – the swinging newspaper cutting in the Norwich Oxfam shop, for instance, the rumpled bedclothes in Sutherland House, Southwold, the design pinned to the wall by Miss Thair which fell on to her bed – but the movements in the grocer's shop were considerable and excessive; quite bulky and heavy items were moved about, items which would require the expenditure of a certain amount of physical energy even from a living human being. How then could a spirit, still less an emotional impression left on the surroundings, possibly effect such physical demonstrations? We are forced at this point to consider that the theory of reception and transmission of impressions may only be *one* explanation for *one* type of manifestation: there may well be others which are less comfortable. The use of energy in whatever form implies the presence of an agency to manipulate it. If the energy's expression be wild and random (as in the case of poltergeist phenomena) then one might say that no intelligence is present, that the energy could be arbitrarily generated or already existing in the surroundings, and that a spontaneous explosion of force might occur as a result.

And if one accepts the last supposition, one must look at what manner of energy would so exist. It could be a form of human energy which is somehow diverted or distorted by unknown means (a theory already considered in connection with poltergeists); or it could be an existent but inert form currently present in the environment. Heat would be one such energy-form.

Presupposing that heat is the energy used to implement physical manifestations, it is likely that any transmutation of it into another form would result in considerable heat-loss in the atmosphere. We have already seen that in almost every case of haunting a drop in temperature preludes the manifestation. QED?

Which brings us to the next point. If energy is used – whether human or abstract – *whose* is the agency responsible for its manipulation?

My thoughts still running along these puzzling and alarming lines, I was not even surprised to learn that yet another shop on the opposite side of Royston High Street also had a reputed ghost. The premises had once been a public-house – the old Angel Inn – and on several occasions the sound of footsteps had been heard in the building. However, so much renovation and alteration has taken place here that the sounds have been lost and assistants in the shops now occupying the site had no knowledge of any unusual happenings recently.

Moving out of Royston, I heard of a haunting on the town's outskirts. The house concerned was built at the turn of the century and is a typically sound Edwardian structure with nothing on the outside to mark it off from a dozen others of its kind. However, one or two occurrences of interest have taken place there.

The owner, Mrs Grayling, stated that a predecessor in the house had told her that one particular room was always very cold. She was asked on another occasion if the room were still haunted, but even now she is not sure whether the answer to that question is affirmative or not.

What she does vouch for is that both she and her daughter have seen an unusual light in the room while they were sleeping in it. Mrs Grayling herself describes it as a round light which appeared above the mantelpiece at a time when there was neither light from the windows nor from any other source. On each occasion the occupant of the room was wide awake at the time, and there was no question of a dream being the explanation.

I have had similar experiences to this myself when a bedroom has suddenly seemed to be illuminated by a light which was neither within nor without the room. On each occasion I attributed the phenomenon either to a state of mind or a state of eyes, and did not seek a supernatural explanation. However, I have seen only a generalised not a localised light. The latter can less easily be explained as physical or psychological illusion.

Travelling south-east from Royston you come eventually to Saw-bridgeworth, a small town which has stories of a haunting. Here a local lady, an archaeologist, with an interest in legend was able to give me information about Hyde Hall. This house is now a girls' school, but at one time was owned by Sir Strange Jocelyn or Joscelyne, member of a family of non-Conformists. (The area was strongly Quaker in the seventeenth and eighteenth centuries.)

Sir Strange's religious views brought him into conflict with the established church in the district, and feeling ran high on both sides. It must have been with a mischievous anticipation of triumph that Hyde Hall's owner suggested that when he died his favourite horse should be buried with him in the local churchyard. He can hardly have been surprised when the scandalised Church authorities refused to agree to the scheme. In course of time Sir Strange Jocelyn and his horse were buried in the grounds of the hall itself.

From time to time Sir Strange apparently reappears, riding up the drive towards his old home. I enquired of several people in the neighbourhood, however, and none knew of any sighting of the ghosts in recent years.

Another story from the distant past comes from Markyate, near Luton, where the spirit of Lady Katherine Ferrers was said to haunt until the middle of the nineteenth century.

Katherine Ferrers had an unusual career, taking to the road as a highwayman in the mid-seventeenth century. She seems to have adopted this role as a result of boredom with her marriage and from then on her life must

*Hyde Hall*

have been as exciting as it was dangerous.

Eventually she was shot at and mortally wounded. She managed to reach the door of a secret room in her house before she died, though by then her secret was out.

After her death the room was bricked up, but Lady Katherine resumed her activities in the form of a ghost riding a phantom horse and revisiting the scene of former crimes.

In 1841 the mansion at Markyate was drastically reconstructed and the secret room disappeared from human knowledge. Since there is no report of a twentieth-century sighting of the lady, it must be assumed that the renovations also removed the ghost.

The phantoms of monks and nuns, as we have seen in earlier chapters frequently appear on the site of their former homes. Hinksworth Place, near Baldock, is said to be haunted by monks. The brothers have been seen to come through a wall, sometimes alone, sometimes in procession, no doubt on their way to and from service through a doorway long since bricked up and forgotten.

At one time a cat belonging to the house would walk forward, purring and rub itself affectionately against somebody, unseen by the house's occupants. Obviously a cat-loving ghost, to whom the animal responded!

Another monk is said to haunt the grounds of the castle in Hertford. This is an odd story about the details of which no one in the town seemed clear. All I could gather was that the ghost walked across the castle green holding an apple in its hand. No doubt this feature had some significance at one time, but its relevance has been lost through the years.

After two or three days of searching for elusive monks and nuns, it was a relief to find a ghost story which was vivid, authentic and comparatively recent.

Mrs Hilda Richmond-Hughes, a cultured and sensitive lady with wide-ranging interests, now lives in rural Suffolk, but just after the last war she resided near Bishop's Stortford. At that time she was accustomed to giving talks and lectures around the villages and had agreed to address a meeting in a village near Stortford.

On the day of her visit, she was met at Bishop's Stortford station by a chauffeur and driven to the house of her hostess instead of to the village hall, being told that the time of the meeting had been postponed to allow another nearby hamlet to join her original audience.

Hilda's hostess greeted her at the door of the house, and she was shown round the place – a well-restored and converted farmhouse. The lady of the house then said she understood Mrs Richmond-Hughes to be interested in crafts and showed her some unusual embroidered pictures, worked in human hair. An interesting though unexpected touch of the macabre.

There was little time for conversation, however. Presently her hostess made an apology and withdrew in order to attend to her husband, who was ill in the house. The lecturer was left alone with instructions to look around and entertain herself. This she proceeded to do.

On entering the room she had noticed an unusual feature about it – a triple-arched entrance above a one-step drop in floor level. She found the atmosphere of the room pleasant and unremarkable.

She had spent some moments inspecting the craftwork left for examination, when suddenly she felt that she was not alone. A feeling of presence grew upon her and she smelled a scent of honey and flowers which she recognised as that of a hair cream used by her own husband and sons.

Before she could turn a voice with an American accent spoke over her shoulder. 'It's kinda cosy, isn't it?' She looked round then and saw a tall man wearing a grey-green uniform standing behind her. She noticed particularly that he had grey eyes. Embarrassed at having been caught scrutinising her hostess's handicraft, Mrs Richmond-Hughes turned away in a fit of shyness. However, good manners compelled her to answer her companion and she turned again to speak to him – only to find the room empty. A little put out, she assumed the American must have retreated from her rudeness through one of the archways.

Shortly afterwards her hostess returned and asked Hilda if she had enjoyed herself. 'Yes,' said the latter, 'but I'm afraid your American friend thought me rather a fool, for he departed.' Her hostess looked puzzled and asked which American she referred to. By this time the two women had walked through the arches on their way out of the room; then Hilda saw facing her on the wall three photographs, one above the other. She pointed to one and said, 'Is *he* staying with you?'

If her hostess had looked puzzled earlier, she now looked positively startled. 'He was killed,' she said, 'in an early morning raid.'

It seems that airmen from the nearby air station of North Weald had been in the habit of dropping in to see the family, treating the place as a welcome home-from-home while posted in England. It was common practice for the boys to drop by in the morning to greet their friends after an early raid. The man in the photograph had been particularly fond of the house and its owners. It was he who had spoken over Hilda Richmond-Hughes's shoulder and said, 'It's kinda cosy here, isn't it?'

As can be imagined, both hostess and visitor were deeply disturbed and moved by the occurrence.

This is one of the visitations which cannot be explained away as an 'impression" haunting. Only a flimsy pattern had been established in these surroundings by the living man and while his happiness in the place could have become imprinted on the material environment, it seems more likely that what Hilda Richmond-Hughes experienced was a manifestation of an individual's survival of death. That there is such a survival of personal consciousness in familiar surroundings – at least for a period after physical decease – I am convinced. This seems to have been one such case. The American had loved the house and its people, had no doubt felt a fleeting security and comfort there in the middle of the insecurity of war. Suddenly, deprived of physical being, his consciousness returned, perhaps, to the last place where it had recognised life as good. Is this fanciful, sentimental, far-fetched? To the disbelievers in personal survival, of course it is. But this much I will say: we cannot *know* that there is no survival, any more than we can know that there is. Both beliefs are a matter of faith only. We may arrive at conclusions from evidence available, but in the end there is no proof either way.

Most of my investigations having been so far conducted in the north of the county, I decided to try the south and drove down to Hertford, Knebworth and St Albans.

Hatfield House is lovely, intact, austere and regal, with centuries of politics and power to make it so. No ghosts walk there so I was assured, and certainly the feeling was as matter of fact as it must have been in the Jacobean days of its completion by the first Earl of Salisbury. If ghosts there are in the neighbourhood, I fancy they prefer the old hall, one wing of which remains standing to mark the place where Elizabeth Tudor was imprisoned, where she was courted by the reckless Tom Seymour, where she heard the news of her sister's death and her own accession. The old hall was part of the palace built by Cardinal Morton, Bishop of Ely, the arch-schemer who plotted Richard III's downfall and played himself on to the winning side when Henry Tudor won Bosworth Field.

But no one knows of a haunting even here, where one might expect to find echoes of great and emotional events. I had to look for humbler premises before I found what I was seeking. The place is known as the Old Coach House and is, I suspect, only a little later in date than Morton's palace, being the oldest domestic building in Hatfield. It is now used as a restaurant.

I was not able to talk to anyone who had had experience of hauntings, but gathered that two ghosts have been seen – one a little girl playing in a room, who disappeared when told to run away. The other is that of a man – tall, dark and with a sad expression. Both manifestations are said to be 'friendly' – though I am not sure I know what is meant by the term in relation to ghosts.

I should like to have learned more about this place and its hauntings, but the house's owner was not at home and the gentlemen in charge, charmingly courteous as Italians always are, spoke insufficient English to understand me and I insufficient Italian to question them. So I left Hatfield little wiser than I had arrived.

Knebworth House is reputed to have a haunting – another mysterious portrait, I believe, the appearance of which changes from time to time. However, when I enquired there, no one knew of a ghost; indeed, the inhabitants seemed a little wistful about it as though ghostlessness deprived them of an amenity. Ghosts, apparently, are something of a tourist magnet and a stately home gains in drawing-power if it has one.

And so on to the web and mesh of traffic thrown out from London; on to Salisbury Hall where Nell Gwynne and Charles II kept each other company. The hall is a charming little mansion, and is reputed to be haunted by the ghost of witty, pretty Nellie. However, the owners were busily preparing for a touring-party which was to arrive the next day; ghosts at that moment were not on their minds, but gardening and decorating the house were. I believe Nell has been seen on at least one occasion, dressed in blue and crossing the main hall.

I was glad enough to escape from arterial roads back to the rural peace of north Hertfordshire. I had heard there was a ghost at Albury, and two or three near Great Hormead. The quiet lanes folded round the car; the motor-hum was replaced by birdsong, the motorway signs by chestnut trees in flower. It was like a homecoming.

It is significant, I think, that the areas associated with ghosts are mainly rural and/or historical. Perhaps the cities are too new and crude, or their inhabitants too busy, or the noises from the present too raucous and demanding to support ghostly echoes. Certainly I have found few hauntings in cities; the most interesting and detailed stories are those from the countryside, echoes of an old and deeply-rooted way of life.

A story came to me from the village of Albury, relating to an old and formerly moated house there. The story's origins are fairly recent, however. In 1926, a woman living at this house, a Mrs Marsh, was found murdered in strange circumstances. There was no clue to her killing save for a broken bottle and an empty crate found on her body. There were extensive police investigations at the time and for some while afterwards, but no arrest was made and the murderer was never caught.

At intervals since then sounds have been heard in the neighbourhood of the house which suggest a re-enactment of the murder. One of the noises is the smashing of glass.

Old villagers who know the place are not keen to go near it at night, though I discovered that younger members of the community seemed to know nothing of the story. Perhaps if some person were courageous enough to investigate the haunting in depth, a clue to the murderer might be obtained – though after fifty years he has probably joined his victim in the bourne from which no traveller returns.

And so back to Great Hormead, to the farm where I spent a happy two days with friends eager to help and to listen to the various stories the researches produced.

The Hormeads, Great and Little, are villages of charm and character, with a sprinkling of ancient houses among the new. An old and lovely house belongs to Mr and Mrs Moon, and they told me an interesting story connected with it. Mrs Moon was not sure whether or not she had a ghost story to tell me, but after hearing details from her and from her daughter, Clare, I am convinced that the Moons share their home with an echo of a former inhabitant.

The deeds of the propery were in the living of St John's College, Cambridge and at one time the house was known as Rectory Cottage. Its date of building is thought to be early sixteenth century and originally the structure was L-shaped. Now only one wing remains, but that is in a good state of preservation and in fact the house is one of the most attractive of its period and size I have seen. Its owners obviously cherish it.

However, there have been times when the Moons wondered if they were truly alone there. All members of the family have heard the sound of footsteps in the upstairs rooms. The steps are heavy, and seem to be those of a male rather than a female. Generally they descend from the attic, although Clare Moon told me of one interesting experience which occurred while a party was in progress at the house. She distinctly heard someone open the front door and go up the stairs, but when she went to look no one was to be found.

A firm named McMullens had been engaged to supply drinks and waiters for the occasion, and one of its most experienced men, named Collins, had been sent to take charge. This man, I was assured by Mrs Moon, is not at all given to superstitious imaginings, but is a downright and eminently sensible person. Early in the evening of the party, Collins was in the kitchen when he heard someone walking about upstairs. He must have been certain at the time that the walker was not a member of the family, because his immediate thought was that some unauthorised person had entered the house. He went up at once, thinking to find either a gate-crasher or an intruder seeking mink coats and other pickings from guests, but to his astonishment there was no one upstairs.

The Moon family are still not sure they have a ghost, but I noticed they referred to it rather affectionately as 'he' and seemed to feel that whatever presence shared the house with them was friendly, and as much entitled to be there as they.

Possibly the haunter was once an inhabitant of the place – since the attic is involved in the manifestations, the ghost could be that of a former servant; but from what period of time there is no means of knowing.

I had heard of a ghost at Brick House near Great Hormead, and went along to investigate, but though the place was an attractive example of Tudor building, and had enough historic atmosphere to generate fifty ghosts, I was assured by the owners that the only resident spirits were in the whisky decanter.

The building is on the site of a Saxon structure, and local legend has it that here Alfred burned the cakes. I had thought the site of this culinary catastrophe was in Wessex. Whatever the truth of that, there seems no foundation for the rumour that the house is the haunt of a monk. Neighbours thought the monk story possibly originated from the shadow-shape of a tree which once stood outside the sitting-room window of Brick House.

So, another non-ghost story from Hertfordshire.

The last story I heard in the county was authentic enough. It was told me by Mr Albert King of Great Hormead. Albert is a great character, getting on in years now, but still with a lively energy and a keen interest in the ways of the world around him. His daughter and son-in-law were the friends on whose farm I was staying and June had promised that her father had a good ghost story to tell. He told me the following tale.

When he was in his late teens Albert King lived at Little Hormead, but belonged to a club at the larger village of Great Hormead. He left the club one night at 10.00 p.m., and came out into the inky blackness which on occasions occurs in the deep country. So dark was the night that he was compelled to travel slowly and by the time he reached Great Hormead Church, he decided to pause for a cigarette. He stopped in the roadway by the churchyard, but hardly had he taken out his cigarettes than he saw a movement in the driveway leading from the road, past the churchyard. He stared, and made out a figure wearing a light garment of some kind. Being a bold as well as an inquisitive lad, he slipped into the chuchyard and stood partially concealed by a yew tree, watching the movements of the figure in the drive.

For some time the thing moved backwards and forwards, from side to side of the drive, as though seeking something. After a while it began to walk towards the tree where young Albert stood in hiding. After a few paces, however (and this must have been a relief to the watcher), the searcher paused and began its side to side scrutiny of the ground as before. The shape walked backwards and forwards, for some time, then retraced its steps to the original position, and in a short while disappeared.

When I asked Albert King how near to him the figure approached he thought that at its nearest it would be about fourteen yards away.

'Was it a human shape?' I asked him.

'Yes, without any doubt.'

'Any particular colour?'

'No. It was just a light shape against the darkness.'

'How exactly did it move? Did it walk? Run?'

Albert shook his head. 'Neither. Smoother movement than that – a kind of gliding. And,' he added, 'it moved steadily.'

So there it was; a seeking ghost. Apparently the spectre had been seen on many occasions in the past. At the time the young Albert King saw it there were several people alive who had witnessed the haunting. I gather nothing has been reported for a considerable time, however, so perhaps no more will be heard of it.

When I asked about the story's origins, I was told that the site was said to be that of a murder, but when and by whom, I could not discover.

I went later to look at the churchyard and the driveway, and found the latter shadowed and gloomy in spite of the sunny day.

Hertfordshire had proved to be a relatively unhaunted county. However, my visit had been a pleasant one and I left the farm laden with plants for my garden and invitations to return soon.

*Great Hormead Church*

# ESSEX
## Fires and Laughter and the Unlucky Witches

Essex, land of the East Saxons, is a county of charm and contrast. It has its cities old and new and these concentrate the industry and commerce of the area. Cities are much the same wherever you go. Rural Essex, however, has the air of not belonging in the same county as the urban areas; there is a timelessness, a feeling that the villages have existed for ever, having grown naturally out of the surrounding countryside and developed their own distinctive characters in their own time, independent of outside influences.

This is not true, of course. The influence of the immigrant Huguenots appears here; there are traces of the woollen and cutlery industries; the countryside has seen a series of invaders come and go – Romans, Saxons, Normans. Yet throughout its history Essex has retained one rich constant – agriculture and the manners and customs of that way of life. There is still something slow, steady, unshakeable in the country people. Their memories are long, their histories fruitful, their wisdom deep. To talk to them is to go back in time to an older, pleasanter and happier England.

There was no need to look for ghosts here; the place is so full of echoes of the past that the stories come up in normal conversation, as though one spoke of near relatives who had been visiting only last week. I had, as it happened, been told of one Essex story before I left Hertfordshire, and by the people who were actually involved.

The licensees of an inn in Nuthampstead, Hertfordshire, had previously run the King's Head in Ongar, Essex, and they had a strange tale to tell of the Essex pub.

The King's Head is the oldest public house in Ongar and is no doubt the kind of place where you would expect to find a ghost. However, neither the landlord nor his wife had considered the matter until the night of the incident concerned.

Both Mr and Mrs Angus awoke during the night, to see a curious greenish light shining under their bedroom door. Thinking the corridor light had been left on, Mr Angus got out of bed to deal with it, to discover on opening the door that the corridor was in darkness.

After talking about it for a while, the couple decided the illumination must be moonlight, and having come to that satisfactory conclusion they fell asleep.

The next morning they mentioned the matter to a relative who was staying with them and who had been sleeping in the next room. She immediately said that she also had seen a light shining under the door.

The three then proceeded to work out where the moon was at that time of the night and month – only to find that it had been on the *opposite* side of the house and could not possibly have shone into the corridor or under their bedroom doors. To this day they have not found an explanation for the occurrence.

I drove into Essex from Hertfordshire by way of Dunmow and stopped at the first inn I came to which looked old and interesting in addition to providing meals. It proved to be unhaunted though picturesque. It was a lucky chance which directed me to the place, however, as serving behind the bar was a young woman whose home is very much haunted.

Mrs Rita Bailey is a pretty, dark-haired girl, with a jolly manner and sad eyes. She lives in a house of seventeenth-century construction in the High Street of Dunmow and finds the place very pleasant now that she has grown accustomed to the ghost.

The fact that the house is haunted first registered when she was laying a carpet shortly after moving in. She had swept the floor before the carpet arrived and when the men brought it into the room she propped her sweeping-brush against the wall. She and one of the men began to lay the carpet, then needing the brush, she turned and said, 'Where's that blooming broom?' Immediately, the brush flew across the room to her. The man working on the carpet saw the incident and was as astonished as Mrs Bailey.

This was the beginning of several unexplained incidents. Frequently when she is away from home, the neighbours see lights in the house. On several occasions she herself has heard the sound of footsteps walking up and down in the corridor of the building but when she investigated has found nothing. Mrs Bailey appeared philosophical about the disturbances, but perhaps this is a question of familiarity.

Other patrons of the pub had overheard part of our conversation, and one volunteered the information that a ghostly cat haunts Northbrook House, near Harlow.

It is amazing how the subject of ghosts provokes conversation. I have noticed that it also provokes strong feelings. Reactions are usually divided between the scoffers, who show utter scorn and derision and a tendency to hold the enquirer up to ridicule; and the firm believer, who has either had a supernatural experience or has other reasons for his conviction. In between is the open-minder who doesn't know but is willing to be convinced. It is

*The King's Head, Ongar*

surprising how often one goes into a peaceful gathering and after throwing down the gauntlet of Ghosts – Fact or Fiction, retires leaving behind a violent argument. The inexplicable appears to generate strong feelings.

The ghost cat story seemed a bit unclear. When it looked likely to develop into the ghost of a woman murdered by her lover then reincarnated as a cat, I lost interest in it. We were hovering on the borders of folklore and drifting away from the ghost story proper.

From Dunmow I moved to Thaxted, quiet, picturesque and with some striking architecture. The church is a superb example of an East Anglian 'wool' church and to sit in the churchyard in its shadow on a warm spring afternoon is to slide quietly back into the leisurely lost past. Indeed, here, as everywhere in Essex, I found a strong sense of the nearness of history and of its continuity. The inhabitants seem to carry an awareness of the past within them. It is not just that they remember what was told them by parents and grandparents, what has been handed down verbally as truth and legend, but that it has some meaning for them. They recognise it as the source of their present lives and as a continual reference point for the enriching of those lives. Believing in the influence of history on the present as I do, this was cheering.

I talked to Mrs Abbs, who was arranging flowers in the church, and she exhibited markedly an empathy with the old ways and traditions. In turn she sent me to Miss Maud Challis, an elderly lady with an extensive knowledge of the town. Miss Challis's mother had lived in one of Thaxted's haunted houses, known as The Cobbler's Cottage, and had thought the place certainly had a ghost, though of what kind I could not discover. Eventually, I understand, the building was exorcised.

The old almshouse cottages in Thaxted are said to be still haunted. These stand in the churchyard and one row is entirely uninhabited. It is in here that lights have been seen occasionally, though what these signify no one seemed to know.

A more interesting story is that of a house at the back of the church which formerly belonged to Gustav Holst, the composer. At one time the property had been owned by a man named Arthur Franklin, whose reputation locally was that of a miser. It was believed that Franklin kept his money hoarded in an alcove in the cellar of his house. Whatever the facts, Mrs Holst apparently heard the sound of carpet slippers flopping up and down the cellar stairs on several occasions and is said to have assumed the wearer to be the old miser resuming his ancient habit.

Another story of the neighbourhood came from Miss M. Pole, a Thaxted bookseller with a shop full of treasures. I spent a pleasant half hour there, browsing and talking to the owner, who possessed a rich fund of information, historical and local.

Henham Rectory is haunted, it seems, by the ghost of an Elizabethan lady, whose portrait hangs in the building. Like Henrietta Nelson's, this is another case of a portrait-ghost association, for whenever the Elizabethan woman's picture is moved, its subject appears. I did not visit this rectory nor that at Tapplesfield where a friend of Miss Pole when calling to collect some books was met by the cleaner, who said she would not go into the house unless her husband was present, as the place was haunted.

A more circumstantial tale comes from Tilty Abbey, between Thaxted and Dunmow, where a headless monk is occasionally seen walking along the road known as Cherry or Chawneth Lane.

*Tilty Abbey*

Tilty Abbey was an ancient foundation of the Cistercian order and was already old when King John's men plundered it in 1215. At that time the monks put up some resistance to the royal activities, as a result of which one of their number was beheaded – whether officially or in the course of the struggle is not known. This must be the origin of the ghost story. Further authenticity was lent to it in 1942, when graves on the site were excavated. In one was found a headless skeleton. There was no evidence that the grave had been disturbed at any time prior to its opening then. It is several years now since the monk was reported to have been seen, but even so the sighting is well within living memory.

A correspondent sent me an unusual 'first-hand' story from Newport, near Saffron Walden. Mrs M. C. Jones's experience was in 1935, when she and her family lived in the hamlet of Stondon Massey between Ongar and Brentwood. Their home was a bungalow on an old estate which had been divided and sold for building development.

The family had a happy life there and Mrs Jones liked the house in spite of the fact that her husband worked away from home during the week. She had the company of her daughter, aged fifteen, and her twin boys of five, and had no worries of any consequence to trouble her.

One night in high summer, possibly July according to Mrs Jones's recollection, she was awakened by a soft sound, as though someone had gently opened her bedroom door. Her young daughter was in hospital at the time, though not seriously ill and it seemed likely that the incomer was one of the twins with a pain or ache or something of the kind. Mrs Jones sat up and waited for the child to come up to the bedside. The bed was of the kind with tallish wooden rails at head and foot and she could just see their outline in the pre-dawn light.

As no little boy appeared, she looked at the door and saw it was closed. It was at that moment that she became aware of a woman standing at the foot of the bed; the figure was shadowy but the costume was unmistakably Edwardian, with a lace scarf around the neck and the face shaded by a large picture hat. The figure seemed to be looking directly at Mrs Jones and she saw distinctly the two hands gripping the bedrail until the knuckles showed white. She was not frightened, and asked the figure 'Who are you? What do you want?' There was no reply and for a few minutes the bed's occupant and the visitor gazed at one another in silence, then Mrs Jones noticed that the door was becoming lighter, until at last it was brighter than anything else in the room. And the ghostly lady was no longer there.

A considerable time after this happening Mrs Jones was serving on the Village Hall Committee and at the end of one meeting she overheard a member call across to another, 'Is that not right, Miss Edith? A ghost walks around Stondon?' The person questioned replied in the affirmative and said that her sister had seen it. 'She appears,' she said, 'at the back gate of the Rectory, walks along Canons Walk and disappears into the wood.'

The Miss Edith spoken to was the youngest of three sisters, whose brother was Canon of Stondon Massey Church. They were all elderly people at the time of this incident, but were the children of a man whose ideas on life seem to have approximated to those of a certain Mr Barrett of Wimpole Street in the previous century. The father had been himself a canon and incumbent of Stondon Massey Church, and had forbidden any of his children to marry. However, according to ther villagers native to the area, his son, Miss Edith's brother, had fallen in love with a local girl, and it was their custom to meet at a spot at the edge of Courtfield Wood, two sides of which formed the boundary to the Joneses' own property; a third boundary was formed by the path to the rectory's back entrance.

Mrs Jones, possibly out of diffidence, shyness or fear of ridicule, did not mention her own experience, but merely said to herself, 'I know where she goes when she leaves the wood.'

Was there a house once where Mrs Jones's bungalow eventually stood? And was the secret young lady returning home after her clandestine meeting? Easy enough to see why she, or her pattern image, continued to appear in the familiar setting of the path and the wood, not as easy to see how she could so conveniently fit into a modern house, even though it were on the site of her own former home. Here, however, I am reminded of my own old home and its curious associations. And so often with these extraordinary occurrences, one thinks one has a theory which fits every case, only suddenly to light upon some incident which casts doubt on the theory, or which will not dovetail absolutely with it.

Mrs Jones had another story to tell me, this time of that lovely little gem, The Crown House, Newport. Although the date over the shell porch is recorded as 1692, the house was founded at least a hundred and perhaps a hundred and fifty years earlier.This is another Home Counties house reputed to have been used by Nell Gwynne and Charles II. Newport's proximity to Newmarket makes this a likely story.

At one time Mrs Jones was friendly with the then housekeeper in the place and the latter told her of an unusual experience she had had there. The owner of the house had gone away on holiday and she was in the house alone. Going up to bed on Christmas Eve, she noticed that her employer's bedroom door stood open. This was unusual enough in itself to cause her to pause, then almost immediately she saw the lower half of a man's body dressed in knee breeches, long hose, buckled shoes and a leather apron. No sooner had she absorbed this phenomenon than it was no longer there and the door was shut fast as usual.

It happened that Mrs Jones had some knowledge of the house and knew that before the property was privately owned it was once an inn called either 'The Angel' or 'The Horns'. The partial-image which the housekeeper saw appears to fit an eighteenth-century innkeeper. We have already examined possible explanations for part-images of this kind and it would be interesting to know if a portion of the immediate surroundings of this landing and bedroom had ever been altered or removed.

Minor stories from other parts of Essex include two from Tollesbury, told me by Steve Carter of Chelmsford. The first concerns Mr Carter's grandfather, who foresaw his own death. At the time of the incident concerned, he was filling a jug of porter, that apparently long-lost beverage, for his wife, when without warning he dropped the jug and began to cry. On his wife's enquiring the cause of his distress, he said he had seen an angel, who said, 'Daniel, Daniel, you will be on this earth two years and no more.' As it turned out, he died at sea exactly two years from the date of this event. What exactly Steve Carter's grandfather saw there is no means now of knowing, but this must have been one of the annunciatory visitations which have been recorded throughout history – a forecast of times to come rather than a recollection of times past. One cannot even begin to guess how such a process works. If you seek for scientific or even semi-scientific explanations of psychic phenomena, then the most puzzling of all must be the prophetic encounter. The only theory which seems to hold out any possible answers is that of the Time Slip, where one accepts that man-made, chronological time is merely one aspect of the dimension, and that it may interlock at certain points with other aspects or cycles of Time:

> Time present and time past
> Are both perhaps present in time future,
> And time future contained in time past.

Thus Eliot, who sensed and tried to apprehend the strange and unknown nature of time.

The second story is slight but belongs to a category of which we have already seen several examples and concerns Mill Cottage in Tollesbury. Here two cousins in one family shared a bedroom, and on one occasion one of them awoke in the night complaining that someone had twisted his arm. In fact no human action of the kind had taken place, and it was assumed by the adults of the house that the occurrence was a supernatural one.

A third story from Steve Carter concerns a cottage on a hill at Little Baddow near Jay's Green. The inhabitants of the cottage regularly heard footsteps walking round the cottage just after 9.00 p.m. on certain nights. Although they had on several occasions gone outside to see if a prowler was about, no one had ever been seen there. The family assumed the intruder might be a local gardener taking a short cut home through their garden, but on asking this man they found that he had not done so. Although once or twice they called out to the unseen walker, there was never any reply and the only manifestation continued to be the sound of footsteps round the house at the same time on each occasion. Nothing was seen at any time, but the timing of the visitation was precise and regular.

This must have been a pattern-haunting again, a recurrence of an often repeated incident – perhaps a labourer returning home late from the fields to the cottage he had once occupied. Nothing more is known of this case and I cannot say whether or not the place is still affected by the sounds.

There are one or two stories from the Colchester area, including one from the rectory at Polstead, where a child of the family living there used to speak of children she had seen playing under the trees; this, however, may be an imaginative creation of playmates from a lonely, sensitive child; not an uncommon occurrence. From the same area there are vague rumours of a monk who walks from the rectory across the fields, vanishing into the garden of Corder's House. The latter is noted because of its association with the Victorian Red Barn murder, but is not apparently haunted or disturbed supernaturally in any way.

But in Colchester itself recent publicity has been given to the exorcism of the Hostel of the Good Shepherd on East Hill. Here noises have been heard inside the building in the neighbourhood of the chapel and on a few occasions a crucifix in the chapel itself has been moved.

The hostel was formerly part of a large Georgian house built in 1818 for a Rev. John Savile; now the building is used as a Diocesan Home for unmarried mothers. Staff and girls in the hostel found the noises worrying and after footsteps had been heard mounting stairs near the chapel, followed by the sound of a door closing, it was decided to hold a service of exorcism. This was performed by the Rev. Eric Turner, chaplain to the hostel and Rector of St James the Great church nearby. Unfortunately the exorcism appears to have been unsuccessful, for apparently the sounds are still being heard in the building. According to the secretary of the hostel committee, these noises, to her knowledge, have been heard for twenty-five years. It has been thought by the staff that they arose from the nature of the building's structure, but if anything so definite can be heard as footsteps mounting stairs and doors closing, the structure must be very unusual.

Haunted inns seem thin on the ground in Essex, so it was surprising to encounter two in one day.

The St Anne's Castle is an ancient inn, medieval in origin. According to local tradition one room in the building is haunted, its occupants having on occasion been disturbed by knocks, bangs, chilly draughts and a feeling of clamminess. They have also been subjected to the not uncommon phenomenon of having the bedclothes unceremoniously stripped from the bed. It seems that in the past dark shapes have been seen and a child's cries heard. According to local folklore again, a child was once murdered in the room in the presence of its mother – a setting sufficiently charged with high-grade emotion to result, one would say, in a strong retention by the surroundings.

When I asked the present licensee, he laughed the matter off, not believing in such things. His wife apparently thought otherwise and had heard footsteps walking about the building, but unfortunately the lady was busy indoors and her husband was too occupied at the bar to call her, so my quest came to an abrupt end over a Cinzano.

The landlord did mention a place farther along the A131, a hamlet (I assume: when I tried I was unable to locate it) called Scrapfaggot Green. The ghost is said to be that of a witch who was burned locally. A large boulder was placed over her grave presumably to prevent any subsequent spirit wanderings. The precautions seem to have been of no avail; the boulder was moved and the witch wanders – some say to haunt the St Anne's Castle itself.

I have no doubt that deep in this medley of folklore, history, tradition and tarradiddle there is a genuine story of human suffering. Down the centuries it has become distorted and overlaid, fragmented and magnified and now the truth is lost. Was the witch the mother of a child, destroyed under her eyes before she herself was burned? Or are these two separate stories? At least one aspect of the tale is true, I think. Scrapfaggot, according to the landlord of the St Anne's Castle, is the local name for a witch. At any rate the 'faggot' part of the name seems to allude to the ghastly pyre our forefathers used as an execution block for women convicted of witchcraft. Further than that one cannot go without more evidence. Essex holds more than one bit of uncomfortable historical England.

For years the name Saffron Walden was associated in my mind with witchcraft. I cannot now remember why, but I imagine I must have read some book as a child which associated the town with the subject. I would therefore not have been surprised to find my ghost story of the area associated with the black art, but such was not the case. The story send to me by Mrs Anne Willis of Bishop's Stortford is mysterious, intriguing, vaguely historical but nothing at all to do with witches – if one can discount the association with fire and burning which that trade carries.

The Willises took over the tenancy of a cottage near Catmere End about 1967, taking a lease of twelve months on the property. It was not so old as country cottages go – just over a hundred years – and was built on the site and foundations of an older pair of wooden structures razed to the ground by fire some time in the nineteenth century.

Before they moved in the Willises were warned by an acquaintance living locally that the place brought bad luck to its inhabitants. They treated this indulgently, not being superstitious people. However, they were to remember the warning as time passed.

It was a fairly typical rebuilding job, recognisably two farm cottages masquerading as one large house. It had, the Willises noticed, one 'bad' and one 'good' end, the bad end making its occupants feel jumpy and depressed, the good end producing the reverse effect.

To begin with the new tenants knew nothing of the site's history. The first hint they had of occupying an unusual property was when they noticed a strong smell of burning, as with wood and heavy smoke, in the area of the staircase. At first only Mrs Willis noticed it, and although both she and her husband checked the electric wiring and leads they found no cause for the smell. Mainly the scorched smell arose in late afternoon or early evening.

The next notification of a deviation from normal came when the Willises' young son, aged four, asked who the lady was who appeared in his room wearing funny clothes. From his description it was apparent he saw a woman in a long skirt wearing a large hat; the woman was frequently seen weeping.

The child's parents did not pay too much attention to this, for at the time there was no thought of any supernatural occurrence, and the little boy was very young. Some time afterwards the family was returning from a shopping expedition in Stortford and was approaching the cottage, when the child said he could see (or had just seen) 'that lady' digging in the garden. Since his parents saw no one in the garden, they began to wonder. A significant fact was that all the occurrences were around the 'bad' end of the house.

And at this point another curious factor should be noted. Where the child saw the woman digging was at a spot beneath the study window – a place where, according to Mrs Anne Willis, no one could even stand long enough to plant anything, because of the abominable smell which emanated from the place. Nothing would grow there, it seems, and the over-poweringly fetid smell had been blamed on a faulty drainage system.

The family kept dogs, and when these were let out at night they invariably barked at the particular place where the child had seen the woman digging and would run indoors with hackles raised and every evidence of fear.

Sometimes also, said Anne Willis, there was the sensation of being watched while in the study.

Another, and distinctly upsetting manifestation, was to hear the sound of children's footsteps running very fast along the landing. At first the Willises thought their little boy was taking a nocturnal trip to the bathroom, but on going up to investigate invariably found the bathroom empty and the child asleep in his bed. This happened so frequently that finally they accepted the sound and ceased checking on their son.

Occasionally Mrs Willis's parents stayed in the cottage, using a room in the disturbed end of the house, in which stood an old wardrobe with a mirror door. Both Anne Willis and her mother experienced the feeling that if they looked in the mirror they would see someone behind them – than which there is no more disconcerting feeling.

On winter evenings when the lights were newly lit and the curtains not yet drawn, the little boy sometimes cycled a few times around the path circling the house. It was then that he reported seeing an engine and a crowd of people looking through a hedge near the church towards their own cottage. The 'engine' at that time can have conveyed little to the puzzled parents.

On another occasion, just before the Willises left the house for good at the expiry of their lease, the child said he had seen children with tongues hanging out and eyes bulging. None of these disconnected incidents made much sense at the time to Mr and Mrs Willis.

A final incident occurred between eight and nine o'clock one night. Mrs Willis stepped out of the kitchen door to feed the animals, and idly shone the torch she was carrying on to the fields at the end of the garden. To her horror in the beam of her torch she saw what she described as another light shining back from the middle of the ploughed field; the empty field itself could be clearly seen around the second light. She ran into the house, but when she returned the light had vanished.

It was not until they had vacated the house that the Willises learned of the fire which had destroyed the earlier cottages. What was it they had experienced? Had the phantom children been burned to death (the running feet, the distorted appearance of their faces as seen by the little boy)? Was the weeping woman their distraught mother? Was the engine in the hedge a fire engine and the crowd of onlookers villagers watching the houses burn?

A poignant and painful story and one which the Willis family are not likely to forget.

However, one of the strangest incidents occurred after they had moved out of the house. They returned just once to the place to tidy up and finish the cleaning so that all would be ready for the next tenants to move in. The house had been locked as soon as they left it and as far as Mrs Willis knew no one had entered it since. In spite of this, on going into the room which had been her son's, she found the fireplace neatly laid with kindling, the wood criss-crossed in the grate. Anne Willis found this the most disturbing manifestation of all. Understandably so. To move wood and lay a fire requires the expenditure of actual physical energy. But by whom?

I think a record of this disastrous fire in the mid-nineteenth century might show that life was lost by the family living in the house at that time.

This kind of story brings the past extraordinarily close to the present and makes the divisions in time seem flimsy if not arbitrary.

As I drove north towards the Suffolk border in a welter of Whitsun traffic under the prematurely scorching sun, I pondered the variety and strangeness of the manifestations I had found in this one county alone. There had been:

(a) a prophetic manifestation (Tollesbury)

(b) the usual ubiquitous footsteps happenings (Little Baddow, Colchester)

(c) life-pattern hauntings (Thaxted, Stondon Massey)

(d) tragic or emotive hauntings (Catmere End, Tilty Abbey)

(e) animal manifestation (Harlow).

This seemed to cover most of the spectrum, and I hardly expected to encounter anything outside these five categories. And in fact the next haunting, from Sible Hedingham, was not vastly different from many others I had come across.

The Bell Inn possesses a haunted bedroom, and the ghost is that of a sixteen-year-old girl with long black, beribboned hair. The pub is at least three hundred years old and when the present licensees, Mr and Mrs Lane, took it over they were warned that the place was haunted. They were inclined to treat the thing as a joke, but certain events have caused them to revise that view.

During their first year they noticed an appalling smell on the staircase, which Mrs Lane likened to the smell of death. After a time this ceased and the next occurrence was in the bedroom itself. Mrs Lane's sister came on a visit and slept in this room, which at the time was not known to be different from any of the others. The visitor was sound asleep when abruptly the bedclothes were ripped off the bed. The next day there was some laughing about the incident, but later when the Lanes' daughter slept in the room and had a similar experience, the family grew concerned.

A medium from Colchester who was friendly with Mrs Lane was called in. She had not been told in advance which was the haunted room, but went straight to it and once inside appeared to be holding a conversation with someone. On coming out she said she had been talking to a young girl with long black hair and that the latter had used the room in her lifetime and having been happy in it wished to stay there.

Apparently the room is always cold, but since the Lanes no longer sleep visitors in it, no one is inconvenienced. The girl-ghost does not wander elsewhere.

The previous landlord had said that the ghost was that of a little old man who knocks on a downstairs door in the night. (I sometimes wonder what ghosts do during the day), but the Lanes have apparently not encountered the second phantom.

If the ghost story at Sible Hedingham was nothing out of the ordinary, the next story certainly was.

I stayed for the night at Finchingfield, partly because I have friends there and had not seen them for a considerable time, and partly because this is one of East Anglia's most attractive villages. It deservedly finds a place on Beautiful Britain calendars, for its combination of old houses, sweepingly curved roadways, little hills and village pond produce an effect which any foreigner or exiled Briton recognises.

I was convinced that here I should find echoes of the past, some stories associated with these ancient lovely buildings. But for twenty-four out of twenty-six hours I spent there no stories came to light save one slight anecdote concerning the Pump House. This had been owned by a former vicar who thought the place was haunted. It seems that the face of an old lady had been seen gazing out of the window, and although I spoke to no one who had actually seen the phenomenon, I was assured that a party of children had done so. Their pet dog had refused to go past the building and they themselves were afraid. However, there was little enough here.

I had paid my bill at the hotel and was on my way out when I chanced to mention the subject to one of the hotel's women employees. As a result I found a story of unusual interest.

Following my conversation with Mrs Pedder, I met and talked at length with her husband, Daniel, and the tale he had to tell was extraordinary.

The Pedders' cottage is situated on the outskirts of the village and is a long, low, thatched structure which looks as though it grew out of the ancient surroundings it stands in.

Inside it was beamed, darkish, inglenook-fireplaced and highly atmospheric. It had been inherited by Mr Pedder through the death of a relative and he and his wife decided to move from the south of England and live in the house. Alterations were required, however, and Daniel Pedder set about doing them himself.

All went normally until he began to rebuild the east wall. Like most old East Anglian houses the cavities between inner and outer wall were filled with rubble and it was while taking out this material that Daniel Pedder came across the stick. He showed the object to me. It was longer than the normal walking stick and bore two curious carvings, a third of the way from each end of the stick. I studied the carvings for a few minutes before I made out their representation. They were meant to be coiled serpents and the coils of one ran in the opposite direction to the coils on the other – one going widdershins, one anti-widdershins.

'What is it?' I asked. 'I've never seen anything like it.'

'It's a witch-stick,' he said. And then at my look of non-comprehension, 'It was used for beating witches. The snakes were a charm against evil.' Gingerly I handed the rosewood stick back to him.

'Was there witchcraft in this village?'

'Certainly,' Daniel Pedder said. 'My family are local people, and they lived in this house for many generations. The cottage was built in 1606, according to the records.'

'But how do you know about the witchcraft?' He looked at me for a moment without answering. Then:

'My great-great-grandmother's sister was beaten to death as a witch,' he said. 'Some time in the late eighteenth century or early nineteenth perhaps.'

He had told the story often enough before to curious enquirers, but was quite willing to tell it again. It seems that the woman had been suspected of witchcraft and had been caught by the villagers in the act of teaching the art to some of the local girls. The event had taken place in that very cottage in which we stood. The woman had been dragged outside and beaten to death by her accusers. Afterwards the 'witch-stick' must have been inserted into the wall as a charm and not discovered until Daniel Pedder had begun his renovations.

'I'll show you something else,' he said. Thereupon he produced a second

*The Pedders' Cottage*

stick, shorter than the first and the length of an average walking stick. The remarkable thing about it was that it was marked down its whole length with intricate designs and patterns which appeared to have been burned into the wood. When I looked closely at the dense design, I had another surprise.

Here was a bull leading three cows; next came a small family of rabbits; there were butterflies, birds, flowers, bees following each other down the slim shaft – everything which symbolises spring and fertility in the mind of Man seemed to have been burned into that stick.

I looked up at Daniel Pedder. 'It's a fertility stick,' I said.

'Yes. And do you know where it was found? Buried in the old thatch right in the middle of the roof between the two chimney-pots. The thatcher found it when we had the roof re-done.'

Mr Pedder thought the stick may have been left there in error by an earlier thatcher, but its exact positioning seemed to me to be consistent with a deliberate planting. Another good luck charm to ward off the evil heritage of the house, perhaps. This placed to guard the roof as the other guarded the walls. Both sticks had been shown to antiquarians locally and in London and Mr Pedder's conclusions were largely based on what he had been told by them.

We had become so absorbed in the historical details that I had almost forgotten the purpose for which I had come. His ghost story seemed to spring naturally from what had gone before.

The garden was not to his liking when he took over the house, and being a keen gardener, he immediately got to work on it. While deep digging one day he approached one of two or three old apple trees and began to dig round it. All went normally until he reached the point nearest the house, when without warning he received a push in the back. Startled, he looked up, thinking someone must have come up unheard behind him. However, he was alone. After a second or two he decided he must have been mistaken in what he thought had occurred and recommenced digging around the tree. When his spadework brought him back to the same area a few minutes later, precisely the same thing happened. He was given a push in the back which sent him off balance. This time he decided to stay on the spot and dig. After a while he came upon two pewter beakers, one larger than the other, buried unwrapped in the soil. He took them indoors, cleaned them and stood them on his mantelpiece.

They were ordinary enough when I examined them, not particularly beautiful, but reasonably neat and well-shaped. One was in better condition than the other.

What is the explanation? There are several possible, I think, but the one which seems to me to be at least probable is that the two pieces were the only objects of value which the original owner possessed and that these were buried in a time of danger with the intention that they be dug up again when the emergency was ended.

But they were never recovered, so what became of the owner? And what was the danger so fearful that the household treasure needed to be hidden?

I thought again of Daniel Pedder's ancestress, caught in the act of witchcraft and knowing that she would be interrogated, her house ransacked and possibly goods confiscated or pilfered. This was the least she could expect for the crime of which she was accused. No time to hide much, no time to go far. She buried her most valuable possessions, the two pewter mugs, in the garden where she could see the spot from her window (an apple tree may or may not have been there at the time) intending to recover them later.

Unfortunately for her, life was at its end the moment the villagers took sticks to her. There was never any question of coming back. The pewter mugs remained where she had planted them. Until her descendant began to dig the garden two centuries later.

A strange tale, indeed. Maybe my interpretation of its components – the sticks, the buried mugs, the motivation, the chief participant – is inaccurate. It makes a reasonably coherent and logical explanation. No one will ever know whether it is wide of the mark or right in the gold.

I drove back into Suffolk by way of the village of Borley. I had never visited the place, but knew something of Harry Price's activities plus those of a ghost or two in the area of church and rectory. I had, besides, heard an interesting tale from Mrs Violet Sorfleet,* now living in Lincolnshire, but born at Long Melford, Suffolk, only a mile or two from Borley. In her letter, Mrs Sorfleet vouched for the truth of the occurrence and said that only three people knew of it; they had all been participants or victims, depending on where you stand in these matters. All three people concerned had been afraid of ridicule, and possibly of the notoriety which had attached to the Harry Price investigation.

In the late autumn of 1939 on an evening of sharp frost, the narrator and a girl-friend were walking along the outskirts of Long Melford when they met a young man friend whom they had not seen for some time. The evening was too cold to stand and talk, so the three decided to walk as far as Borley Rectory, a matter of a mile and a half distant. The rectory had been burned down in February of that year and they thought to look at the ruins of the place.

Like many of the people living in the area, they were sceptical of the current stories of ghosts at Borley, and suspected that the frequent sightseers to the place 'were a bit soft'.

They were all very young – eighteen, twenty and twenty-one respectively – and were laughing, chatting and fooling around as they walked. The night was bright, cold and clear in the autumn moonlight, and when eventually they reached the rectory there seemed little to see; a pile of broken walls, burnt timbers and rubble, stark against the sky. The three young people leaned on the five-barred gate at the entrance to the drive and discussed the matter. Someone remarked that it looked ordinary enough and what was all the fuss about? Then, to quote Mrs Sorfleet, 'out of nowhere came the most evil, filthy presence. We were surrounded by a moist, misty *something*, which hid us from each other and terrified us. My hair stood on end, and I leapt off the gate and ran like hell to some cottages about a mile away; the four minute mile wasn't in it.' The sound of laughter followed her down the lane as she ran.

Her friends had also bolted and it was some time before any of them had recovered sufficiently from the fright to analyse what had happened. In fact no analysis was possible. They asked each other what it was they had experienced, but no one had an answer to the question.

Does the ghostly laughter suggest a living practical joker? Possibly, but the mist, the sense of evil, do not. Mrs Sorfleet interestingly uses the word 'filthy' to describe what was experienced. The sensation of infinite corruption and defilement is often associated with evil. It is also associated with a certain type of psychic manifestation known as an elemental. I suspect that the latter are concentrations of fairly primitive emotion. They invariably seem to be thoroughly unpleasant.

I arrived in Borley full of curiosity, expecting some dark ancient village bristling with strange forces. I found an open sunny little hamlet, attractive houses scattered along its principal lane and an elderly woman placidly gardening outside of one, her cat playing round her feet. She did not believe in Borley's ghosts, neither did a young lad I met outside the ruins of the rectory.

As for the latter nothing is to be seen there save weeds and grass hummocks which may or may not conceal masonry. I stood by the fence and looked over, but saw and heard nothing. One never does when one is searching. But that is not only true of ghost-hunts.

# NORTHAMPTONSHIRE
## A Pail, a Queen and a Voice from the Middle Ages

I had always regarded Northamptonshire as a county one passed through en route from somewhere else; territory largely unknown and, by implication, of little interest to visit. After all, what did one know of it? The shoe industry at Northampton town, steel at Corby, one (or was it two?) of the great fenland rivers, the site of Fotheringhay Castle where Scots Mary was done to death, the famous school at Oundle – these were part of the simple image which the word Northamptonshire conjured. When I visited the county to enquire about its ghosts, I had the surprise of my life; it was like walking to a backdrop of stage scenery only to find that behind it lay the real thing – woods, rivers, streams, meadows, old halls and houses – a mellow world and landscape, housing a people of warmth, hospitality and interested friendliness.

The north-east of the county, though near the fen city of Peterborough, retains a strongly individual character and as yet its placid pastoral landscape and way of life seem uninfluenced by industrial threat or motorway development. I say 'seem', but the threat is there.

Dormitory development is beginning to take place in the Oundle area and it may not be long before these secluded and beautiful villages lose their character, crumble from the dignity of Tudor stone and thatch to the uniformity of tile, brick and ferro-concrete.

To walk into villages like Warmington, Barnwell, Ashton, Fotheringhay, is to step back through the mirror of one's own times into an older concealed world, where transport was by horse, milking was by hand, butter was by courtesy of the farmwife and local celebrations were the county fairs or maypole dancing. Somehow a flavour of all these has been left behind. In the slow summer days a richness had accumulated which was composed partly of memory, partly of heredity and partly of pure good temper. The people of Northants, *like* their countryside and belong to it much as do their trees and rivers. Many of the inhabitants come from families who have lived in the same area of the county for centuries.

When I asked one young man – talented and normally ambitious – if he would like to live elsewhere, he replied that he preferred to stay in rural Northamptonshire. After travelling around the county for a while I could understand why.

I stayed at The Ship in Oundle, and its owners, Mr and Mrs Franklin and Mr Ian Fleming (no relation to the other of that name as far as I know), had only had the place for eighteen months. The usual renovations had begun to take place, during the course of which they had found a magnificent inglenook fireplace and a ghost story. The inglenook is, I hope, a permanent feature; the ghost has proved more ephemeral.

The inn is a seventeenth-century structure, but the origin of the ghost story stems from recent times. A former landlord committed suicide by throwing himself from the window of a bedroom and it is said that a previous licensee and a sometime guest at the inn both had the experience of someone unseen brushing past them on the stairs.

Ronald Franklin, when he first moved into the place, slept in the haunted room, knowing nothing of any haunting. In fact 'slept' is an inaccurate description of his night's lodging in bedroom No. 1. He was unable to sleep all night owing to a feeling of disturbance and unease, which at one point brought the hair prickling along his neck. Children who were later put in the room, also in ignorance, also failed to find sleep. They stated, with the illogical conviction of the young, that it was 'full of demons'.

I looked into Room No. 1 and found in it the curious restless, disturbing quality which often remains after a haunting has ceased to operate in an area. One is left with unease, a back-wash of the active and inexplicable.

I met this particular sensation in several places I visited in the neighbourhood and many of the stories were of ghosts which had not been encountered for ten years or more. I suspect that after so long a lapse of time a haunting may be said to have ceased or at least to have weakened beyond the strength when it can be detected by human sensitivity.

One such could have been the noted Drumming Well of Oundle, had not the explanation for its current inactivity been that the structure has been filled in. For two or three hundred years this well emitted the sound of drumming as a warning of portentous national events. Admittedly there were intervals of several years between manifestations, but then national calamities, such as the passing of kings (the well drummed before the death of Charles II) do not occur weekly.

Various psychic theories were put forward for the phenomenon until the hot air was displaced by a scientific explanation – *viz.* that 'the sound was caused by air being expelled through compression from the rock crevices into the well'. Scientific? I do not know if such an explanation is viable, but this tale smacks more of the practical than the psychic in all its aspects.

Northamptonshire people are refreshingly open-minded on the subject of hauntings. The area is so plentifully stocked with ghost stories that it would be foolish to be out-and-out sceptical. I found several examples of persons who had originally laughed at such stories, but whose subsequent experience had turned derision into doubt and doubt into admission that 'there are more things in heaven and earth, Horatio . . .'

One such was Violet Rimmer, a freelance journalist, who worked for a while in 1967 in a shoe store in Northampton. Vi Rimmer was far from gullible and treated stories of a ghost with scepticism. However, two other assistants in the shop assured her that the haunter was male. The three women, with more valour than discretion, then began to try to contact the ghost by way of a home-made Ouija board. This is, in my view, quite one of the most dangerous games to play and those who indulge in it are likely to get more than they bargain for.

In this case, the girls 'contacted' an entity called William, who had owned a butcher's shop on the site in Elizabethan times. It seems his young son, Adam, also remained with him in his state of limbo. According to the Ouija announcements, William had hidden vital deeds to his former property and these had been lost. He appeared to need their recovery and recognition before he could leave the scene of his earthly existence.

The ghost appeared to Vi Rimmer on several occasions – one, alarmingly, as the gigantic shadow of a huge man. His presence was also manifested by an icy coldness, 'like standing next to a thick block of ice'.

When the property underwent repairs, various hidden passages and cavities were revealed, but the assistants' searches for the missing papers were less thorough than they would have wished. They were deterred by the cobwebs, spiders, and generally unsavoury nature of the new discoveries. So William's secret remained lost, his plea for help unanswered. Violet

Rimmer's health began to be affected by the conditions under which she was working and she shortly left her employment. She learnt later that the ghost still frequented the place, but less often than formerly. This, apparently a real survival-after-death haunting, is an example of the gradual lessening of manifestations over a long period of time. If one accepts the theory of death-survival of the individual, then it seems that the surviving intelligence slowly becomes aware of a different set of circumstances from those his conscious mind knew in life. Or of no circumstances? Do the surviving dead, if such they be, move on to other existences or do their separate spirits lose individuality by degrees until at length they are reabsorbed into some nameless, unimaginable whole, the stream of consciousness, the general pool of awareness which informs 'life'?

As many questions can be asked in relation to the 'broadcast' theory of haunting. Does the power of the imprint or record lessen with time? No matter what theory one arrives at in relation to ghosts, proof is unobtainable; all must be speculation, guesswork. It is, I suppose, good to have some mysteries left in this age when most aspects of life are stripped to their bones and exhibited publicly.

Some of the Northamptonshire ghosts have defied analysis in spite of considerable publicity. One such is the spectre of Salcey Forest, which occasionally seems associated with a second ghost. The most frequently seen is the figure of an exceptionally tall man, dressed in black cloak and hood (monk's habit?) gliding very fast across a stretch of cornfield on the forest's edge.

Apparently Salcey Forest has had a reputation for being haunted for as long as the local inhabitants can remember, and they speak of hauntings in the time of their fathers and grandfathers in the area. The ghostly monk, if such he was, is one of the regular apparitions.

A local tradition states that after the Restoration of the monarchy in the seventeenth century, Charles II took a nearby house for a time in which to house Mistress Eleanor Gwynne. (Nell seems to have travelled widely once she acquired a royal lover.) Salcey Lawn was isolated in the middle of the forest and Nell grew bored and restless when her lord was absent. So bored that she acquired another lover. Charles was not pleased to be cuckolded and, so rumour states, had the luckless man murdered; since when the latter is seen hurrying through the forest, on what desperate errand none can guess.

The second apparition is said to be that of Nell herself. She has been seen on several occasions seated in the orchard of her former home. It has even been hinted that King Charles once walked in the house of Salcey Lawn, but extensive renovations seem to have removed this haunting.

The historical tale is attractive though smacking strongly of fiction. Would Charles have had a sexual rival murdered? It would have been an uncharacteristic activity for him, since he was one of the few Stuarts with a sense of humour. Much more likely that he would have laughed the matter off or found an amusing way to humiliate his rival.

The sound of a carriage and horses has also been heard – though not seen – in the forest from time to time.

A story of a more fragmentary nature is associated with Dallington Church, and as far as I am aware the ghosts were seen only once, though by two people in succession.

The church is thirteenth century, heavily restored and the incident in question took place in 1907, when two young girls visited it at the end of a country walk from Harlestone Firs. It was dusk and about eight o'clock in the evening when the girls arrived at the church. One of the two was on a visit to the other, her home being in Kent. It was the local girl who first went into the building, though she came out again almost immediately. The visitor, curious to see what had caused her friend's panic and not waiting for explanations, pushed past her and into the church. She found the place full of kneeling people, but they appeared, as she said, 'to be made of a substance similar to bubbles'. No explanation has ever been proffered for what the girls saw, and apparently the phenomenon has not recurred since that time. The Kentish girl, now an elderly woman living in Berkeley, California, tried a few years ago to discover an historical origin for what she and her friend encountered, but without success.

This is a curious but tantalisingly abortive glimpse of the supernatural. Another Dallington story is more in line with the usual pattern of hauntings. It was told me by Mrs Aileen Bullock and concerned her schooldays. She was a pupil at Dallington School (the building is no longer used for this purpose) and was about nine years old at the time. She and other girls had discussed the story of the Grey Lady who supposedly haunted Dallington Church, and who was thought to be the spirit of a former Lady Spencer.

Aileen and a friend were curious enough to try to see the ghost and on their way home entered the churchyard. They descended a flight of steps into a passageway and as they reached the bottom step 'a figure wearing a flowing grey cape rushed by'. The foremost child (Aileen) screamed and turned to run, but states that she 'kept slipping back as if some force was pulling me'. The second girl apparently reached the top well ahead and had seen nothing.

Mrs Bullock vouches for what she saw, but certain aspects occur to me for consideration. In the first place, the pupils had *as a group* discussed the ghost and the Grey Lady's prompt appearance suggests a practical joke. Yet if this were so, the joker would almost certainly have revealed herself soon afterwards. The essence of practical jokes is that the jokee shall know he has been had.

In the second place, a child of that age with a lively imagination and some sensitivity could have conjured up what she expected (dreaded? desired?) to see easily enough.

In the third place, the timing of the appearance so soon after the discussion is a strong coincidence.

Yet with all this taken into consideration, there is a fragrance of the inexplicable here. The church *did* have a legend, it seems, though Mrs Millicent Lawrence of California was unable to find it. And the two girls in 1907 apparently had an encounter with some kind of psychic phenomenon. Young Aileen Barker's experience appears to have been very real to her and has stayed in her memory vividly into maturity.

Northamptonshire has more than the usual share of haunted churches and apparently less than its quota of haunted pubs. Of the latter, one which has carried its past actively into the present is the Black Lion at Northampton.

There is a long record of haunting here – the inn itself is ancient, being known before 1720 as The Plasterers' Arms. A succession of landlords in the present century have had 'experiences', predominant among them being the switching on and off of lights, the sound of footsteps, shadows passing behind glazed doors and on at least two occasions actual apparitions. Sometimes there are variations, such as the night when an eighteen-gallon barrel of beer was moved from the ramp into the gangway of the cellar without a sound being heard by any occupant of the house.

The stories run roughly as follows. During the tenancy of Mr Robert Brewer, who was licensee in the mid-1960s, the incident of the beer barrel took place. Prior to this the Brewers had had trouble with the house lights. They would switch off at night, only to find in the morning that a number of lights were still burning.

A local resident, Mr B. Hall, who knew the pub well, had several times heard footsteps passing along corridors and sounding overhead. When investigated, no human agency appeared to be responsible. He also had seen shadows moving behind glass partitions, with no one there.

Beneath the inn are cellars, one a vast square with stone walls and an ancient vaulted roof. This appears to be an area of especial concentration for phenomena. Animals shun this cellar and dogs coerced by their owners into accompanying them into the place have shown extreme fear and reluctance. Several licensees experienced a feeling of chill and discomfort in this part of the building. On one occasion vapour was seen – 'like a fog or mist' – arising from one corner of this cellar. It remained for a few minutes then disappeared.

Almost all the recent licensees have had trouble with the lighting system. Even after checking and re-checking that lights were switched off, the bulbs have been found burning the following morning. And on at least one occasion a part of the system refused to operate though it was later found to be perfectly in order.

One former licensee, a Mr Timothy Webb, had the Black Lion for four years, and during that time underwent the usual run of experiences plus one of greater significance. He was in his bedroom one evening and suddenly found himself looking at a man of heavy build with a large black dog beside him. He had roundly told the man to get out before he realised the dog was not his own dog and that what he was seeing was not there, was not flesh and blood. For a few minutes afterwards he doubted his sanity, which is hardly surprising.

Some time later in discussion with a friend, Timothy Webb's wife revealed that she had passed on the stairs a woman in a riding-habit. There was, of course, no such person present.

Other licensees heard and saw door knobs rattling, and one, Mr James East, tells the story of a Christmas party in the 1950s when guests proposed a séance, causing great disquiet and distress to one man in the party who protested against the idea, saying that he knew 'something was there'. The idea was dropped.

And the hauntings go on. The most recent news from the Black Lion concerns the activities of a Northampton Psychical Research Society who have spent two nights in the affected cellar. The first occasion proved barren but on the second lights were seen moving at the far end of the cellar, in that section reputed to be haunted. The members of the society apparently sat with the electric light on during the greater part of every hour, but for ten minutes in each hour, sat in darkness. It was during one such dark period that the flickering light, akin to candlelight, was seen in the haunted area. The phenomenon lasted only a few seconds, but during that time two of the members present thought they saw a shadowy figure cross the end of the cellar.

The Lion has a new licensee, Mr Terry Canning, who has already received his psychic baptism. Recently he heard the sound of a baby crying. It might have been the Cannings' own baby if it were not for the fact that the latter was fast asleep in her bedroom. There was no other infant in the pub.

On a recent Sunday night Mr Canning went to bed after a hard and tiring day. Usually each night before retiring he switched off the gas cylinders in the cellars. On this occasion, the duty slipped his mind. When he went down to the cellars the next morning, the cylinders had been switched off. This has happened on one subsequent occasion.

The Black Lion is a much haunted pub it seems. But who are the haunters? Or from what is the pattern descended? The only tragic story is that of a murder for which a certain Andrew McRae was sentenced to death on Christmas Eve 1892. The story is ugly enough. McRae is said to have murdered his mistress, Annie Pritchard, and boiled her head and some of her bones in the copper in which he prepared bacon for sale at Northampton market. Their baby also disappeared on the night of the murder. In spite of this, the twentieth-century licensees consider the ghost friendly. I suspect they have more than one ghost.

Of great help to me in my enquiries in the Northampton area was Mr Tony Freeman, a young journalist as interested in psychic phenomena as I. He told me a tale from a village near Corby, concerning a local girl who died in childbirth in a field. None knew for certain the father of her child, but three men were suspected as possibly responsible. In turn each of the three men disappeared and was later found buried in mysterious circumstances. Yet it is the girl whose ghost has been seen walking across the field to the church.

It was Tony Freeman also who drew my attention to the story of Haunt Hill House at Weldon. Built in 1636, the place was once a hostelry for travellers through Rockingham Forest and at some point in the house's history one of its occupants committed suicide in the attic. At intervals since then, bloodstains are said to have appeared on the stairs (or on the doorstep, there seems to be some doubt about location), indicating the place where the suicide's blood dripped after the event. I have not been able to trace any eyewitnesses of this phenomenon.

A story less ghoulish but more interesting concerns the site of the Civil War battle of Naseby. It is said that for about a century afterwards the villagers would congregate on a nearby hill on the anniversary to witness a re-enactment of the battle. The curious feature of this manifestation was that apparently the whole scene took place *in the sky* and the watchers heard cannon fire, saw men fighting and falling, cavalry charging, banners waving, and even heard the screams and groans of the injured as the battle progressed. The sightings seem to have been well known at the time and the stories have been handed down from one generation to the next until they form an unshakeable local tradition.

I am curious about this complete replay of a full-scale event. This is a haunting of a very different kind from the individual ghostly knockings and walkings which abound. The Naseby phenomenon seems to be a 'recorded' manifestation, the strength of which lasted for a number of years, but eventually died out. But recorded by what? And why should the manifestation be aerial in nature?

One might answer the first question with another: what better recorder could there be than the ground over which the battle was fought? And if the battleground itself were to re-broadcast what would be its most likely screen?

It is a pity the manifestation no longer occurs. I'd have been interested to see Cromwell's cavalry in action, after encountering them at peace in Eynesbury.

The village of Foxton is also a haunted area, the rectory apparently being almost as pestered as the former rectory at Borley. Foxton's ghost took the form of footsteps, clanking sounds, mysterious lights and an unidentified figure in a black cloak who habitually walked past a window. Matters came to a head in 1958 when a young couple wished to buy the derelict rectory. A national magazine obtained permission to photograph the building before and after renovation. The photographer printed the shots, only to find that human figures appeared in the print where no figures had been when he took the pictures. In addition, one picture showed a window in a room where there should have been no window.

The upshot was the arranging of a séance at which it is said the ghost of a girl appeared, by name Mary Stanton. Later the investigators elicited the information that she had been killed in a time of religious persecution. Having been accused of some crime or other, she was pursued by the villagers to the rectory, where she sought sanctuary. Sanctuary or no, she was attacked, hit on the head and died as a result of her injuries.

No more is known about the tale, and the village of Foxton is now totally derelict, I understand. Many small hamlets in the county have suffered this fate, in earlier days due to the high incidence of endemic plague in the county and later, in the nineteenth century, as a consequence of the industrial revolution.

Another haunted rectory is at Pilton, a house connected with the Tresham family, whose ancestor was one of the Gunpowder plotters. The ghost was that of a Jesuit priest; I use the past tense because nothing has been heard of this spectre for a considerable time. At one period the family suffered continual disturbances from loud thumpings and bangings which occurred at night. Occasionally a grey figure was seen looking out from a window, and on a few occasions when the house was empty, neighbours perceived lights in the building.

The source of the trouble was located when heating pipes were being laid in the rectory. On taking up a certain section of floorboards the skeleton of a man was found. I do not know how the identification was arrived at, but the investigators concluded that he had been a Jesuit priest who had died where he lay, probably when concealed there to avoid discovery. Immediately one's mind concerns itself with the activities of the persons who hid the man. Would they not have returned to release him? If they found him dead by suffocation or starvation on their return, would they not have given him Christian burial?

It seems the latter was permanently denied him, for the heating engineers who found the skeleton calmly laid their pipes around him and left him where he was. Since then the rectory at Pilton has been quiet. Curiouser and curiouser.

An even odder story, smacking more of magic than a good honest haunting concerns the Face in the Pail. This story is well known in Northamptonshire and received wide publicity throughout the county in 1948.

The tale concerned Mrs Margaret Ellen Leatherland of Teeton, who died in 1967. Her brother, Sir Robert Fossett, had been ill during the winter of 1947–8 and entered hospital in the February. About a month before this date, Mrs Leatherland was milking a cow in the cowshed of the family farm, when she saw on the top of the bucket and framed in the milk-froth, a man's face – the face of her brother.

She came to no hasty conclusions, but took the pail outside and examined it closely; the face remained where she had seen it, and was undoubtedly that of her brother Robert.

According to her account at the time, the incident recurred the next day when she was milking and for several days consecutively. By the fourth or fifth day, she determined to brave ridicule and called her husband and other members of the family. All saw the picture in the pail and none could give an explanation.

The bucket was scrubbed and scoured, but no matter how mercilessly it was cleaned the face reappeared.

By now the tale was around the villages and scoffing unbelievers demanded proof. Mrs Leatherland had photographs of the Face taken and circulated to members of the Fossett family, with what result is unrecorded.

Various outsiders inspected the unusual bucket, including a local reporter, Mr G. B. Freeman, and the then President of Northamptonshire Psychic Society, the late Mr T. Hardiman Scott. Scott said he had seen nothing like it in all his twenty-five years' experience of psychic research!

Whatever the origin and meaning of the Face in the Pail there were two interesting codicils. Three months after the first appearance of the picture, Sir Robert Fossett died; soon after the story was published in the local press, the mysterious bucket disappeared. The enigma was never solved. A possible explanation was put forward that the rough surface of the pail's interior was responsible for the phenomenon. However, this was examined, and although discoloured in places was not thought to be the cause of the formation of the features. If this is truly a psychic rather than physical phenomenon, then I think it must be classified under the heading of prophetic manifestation.

The human face like the human name appears always to have had mystical significance to the mind of man. In primitive societies both were concerned with the soul's representation, the soul's secret. Damage one or the other and the soul would be in jeopardy (by 'soul' the primitive meant that indefinable part of his life which supplied motivation and identification – which was 'I' and not 'he' in relation to the rest of the world). So arises the savage's fear of photography. 'Steal my face and you steal my soul.' Or of speaking the true and proper name of an individual, 'Use my true name and you have power over my soul.'

The single manifestation of a human face, therefore, has a potent effect on a certain part of human receptivity. It is 'significant', powerful, dramatic and accepted as a kind of personal address, if not revelation, to the witness.

One such story concerned a man named Wright, who had come to Gidding village in an attempt to trace his ancestors. He was directed to the church, in the yard of which were buried several members of his family. The man located a headstone bearing his family name, and noted the carving of a cherub with spread wings and puffed-out cheeks at the top of the stone – a conventional graveyard device in the last century. He gazed for a few moments at the carving, and then saw with astonishment that it had taken on the likeness of his grandfather.

This may or may not be a ghost story. I am inclined to think that the face was produced by Mr Wright's subconscious and superimposed upon the stone carving. Or perhaps there was enough likeness between cherub and grandfather to make the transposition of features a logical one. On the other hand, the witness's subconscious may have had nothing to do with the matter, and the metamorphosis may have been an actual psychic manifestation. I hesitate to apply the latter term to any occurrence where a strongly-possible factual explanation exists.

About the next story, which also concerns the appearance of a human face, there can be no doubt. It concerns a Mr Berry, who at the time of which I am writing was a member of the staff of Oundle School.

The teacher at that time was living at Elton and had a room in an old house there. He had returned to his lodgings after school and gone up to his room. Shortly after entering, he was astonished to see on the floor of the room what appeared to be a ball of mist. As he watched it, it began to roll. The teacher watched the thing with horrified concentration. It rolled around the floor for a while then moved up one of the walls until it came to the mantelpiece. There it stationed itself and gradually began to form into the face of a man. The face was terrifyingly real and exceedingly evil in expression. It gazed at Berry for a few minutes, then faded. The manifestation was remarkable for being in colour. Most ghostly appearances are monochrome, variations on grey.

One can imagine few less pleasant experiences than this. As far as I know no explanation for the occurrence was forthcoming.

Oundle town has a good heritage of ghosts. The following incident occurred in a flat occupied by Mr J. Priest and his family at a time when Mr Priest was also on the staff of Oundle's public school.

The Priests' flat was above an empty shop, and the whole premises were very old. The only entrance was through a stone paved yard and the view from the kitchen window took in the entire approach to the building.

Mr Priest's sister was staying with them at the time, and one day while his wife was at work in the kitchen, her sister-in-law came into the room and said that an old-fashioned gentleman with red cheeks and a tall bowler hat was standing by the door, smiling, having apparently arrived to speak to the mistress of the house. Mrs Priest was momentarily nonplussed, wondering how the man could have approached the back door without her having seen him cross the yard. She went out, however, to speak to the stranger, but could see no one at the door. Her sister-in-law continued to see the apparition for several seconds until it melted away.

The Priests later made enquiries locally and found that the ghost's description answered that of a watchmaker who had lived in the house many years before.

John Priest had another story to tell – a story which has its parallels and echoes in many other places, but which is enhanced by the associations of its setting.

Between Oundle and Peterborough lies a village whose name for centuries was significant in English history. Fotheringhay, Fodringeia of Domesday, was an enclosure or 'hay' of Rockingham Forest, and used as a deer enclosure in the winter months. The land, with the castle which was built on it, passed through many ownerships, with frequent reversions to the Crown whenever the currently occupying family lost its luck. Eventually the fortress became permanent Crown property.

The castle has its own story and its ghosts, but John Priest's tale concerns the church at Fotheringhay.

It is an impressive building, the lantern tower carrying its height well above the surrounding marshes to give a clear landmark for several miles around. The body of the church has a lightness of construction which creates an impression of delicacy and the size and number of the windows add to this.

The church has a long past, also, but owed the greater part of its construction, plus the college once attached to it, to the patronage of

*Fotheringhay Church*

Edmund Plantagenet, surnamed Langley, fifth son of Edward III. In turn his son Edward, Duke of York, added to the church, but died at Agincourt on Friday, 25 October 1415. His body was brought back to Fotheringhay and buried in the choir of the church. Later periods of history superimpose themselves. Richard, Duke of York, and his wife, Cecily Neville, 'the Rose of Raby' – parents of Edward IV and Richard III – are buried here. It was Edward who gave the church its beautiful pulpit still in use. Richard, the maligned and much-slandered Richard, was born at the nearby castle and must sometimes have attended service here. Tradition asserts that as a young boy he followed his father's body to its interment at Fotheringhay church.

But the echoes the church carries are of the earlier Plantagenets, and to catch these we must return to the story of Mr and Mrs John Priest.

Some years ago the Priests set out on a walk from Oundle to Fotheringhay, being particularly fond of the old village. They passed the towering grass mound which is all that remains of the castle and went on to the church. It was a still hot day, the village wrapped in the silence of high summer. They turned into the driveway leading to the church, when, to their astonishment they heard music coming from within the building. It was not even of the kind normally associated with the contemporary church service, but was the sound of drums and trumpets. Mrs Priest remarked to her husband that there must be a concert in progress and they should enter quietly.

As they opened the church door the music ceased. They rested a while in the cool of the interior then returned home.

Some time later Mrs Priest's sister and brother-in-law visited them. The Priests took their guests on a tour of local places of interest, ending at Fotheringhay. Later the same evening John Priest's sister-in-law found that she had left her handbag in Fotheringhay Church, and the male members of the family went off by car to recover it. A cleaner at the church told the men that the police superintendent had left with the bag only a few moments earlier and that they might overtake him as he was on foot. This they did and gave the officer a lift back to Oundle. En route he remarked that he rarely walked to Fotheringhay, but on this occasion had wanted to investigate the strange music which people claimed to have heard there. It appeared that his own police sergeant was one of the persons who had experienced the phenomenon.

I asked John Priest about the music, seeking to discover if it were associated with Mary, Queen of Scots. His answer was in the negative. It was not, he thought, of Tudor type but was harsher, more primitive. He associated it with the Agincourt period of Fotheringhay.

What commemoration was this, I wonder, that it should last so long in time? Edward, Duke of York, son of Edmund de Langley and grandson of Edward III, died at Agincourt and was buried in Fotheringhay Church. With what celebrations? With drums and trumpets, perhaps?

Echoes, echoes; music is the most haunting of all.

Churches occasionally produce this type of phenomenon. I experienced something similar in a Norwich church, and another Northamptonshire church – that at Lutton – produced music for a young man who waited outside it. This man heard the organ playing as he approached Lutton Church. My own experience was to hear the organ playing as I stood *inside* St Andrew's Church in Norwich. In neither case was any organist present nor any actual instrument being played.

As I talked to people in the county, I was astonished by the number of minor hauntings mentioned. If conversations began with a major story, they invariably ended with two or three small ghosts thrown in for good measure.

Did I know, I was asked, about the ghost of Delapre Abbey (once De la Pré)? This was a librarian said to appear occasionally. Or had I heard of the nun at Notre Dame Convent School in Northampton? She habitually walked knee-deep through the floor of a room, the floor now being raised a foot or so above its original level. Had I been told of the farmer at Marhon who smells arum lilies in his house each year before the feast of Corpus Christi? I had not, but my questions revealed that the house stood on former abbey land.

There was a story of Rushton Hall, near Kettering, said to be haunted by the ghosts of a horseman, his horse and his black dog. (I wonder why brown dogs don't haunt, or golden retrievers. Dog spooks always seem to be white or black.) In this particular case, an extension wing was planned on the side of the house where the ghosts had been seen. When the labourers began to dig, they unearthed the skeletons of – a man, a horse and a dog. A hunting gentleman, I should say.

There are ghosts at Milton Malsor, connected with an ancient house of monastic history. Local people say that ghostly figures have been seen passing from the drive of this house, across the lane and into the walled footpath opposite. After a few paces, the monks (for such they are) turn left and walk through a bricked up doorway into the grounds of a neighbouring large house.

A local schoolgirl, while doing an early morning paper round, once saw a white figure in the garden of Milton House. This became translucent as she approached, then faded away.

A modern haunting takes place on a road near Towcester, where a phantom lorry drives. This spectre is more harmful than most since it constitutes a driving hazard to other traffic. There have been one or two accidents as a result of the vehicle's being seen.

Sometimes the most unlikely buildings acquire a ghost – for example, the Lyric Bingo Hall at Wellingborough. The explanation here may be that the Lyric is built on the site of an old burial ground. Whatever the reason for the choice of venue, the place is apparently haunted; cupboard doors have swung open, a misty shape has been seen crossing the balcony and lights have also been observed. Matters became interesting enough in 1969 to call for the investigations of a psychical research society from Hertfordshire. It is alleged that their efforts to contact the haunter were successful, though they do not seem to have elicited much information, apart from the fact that the ghost knew he or she was lost and was personally concerned about someone named Daniel. Apparently replies to the society's questions were tapped out, with the aid of some kind of alphabetical system which enabled the spirit to spell its answers.

This is much the same principle as Ouija, and in my opinion this kind of activity is best left alone. I am not superstitious in the sense of feeling that attempts to contact the dead bring ill-luck; but I do believe – and increasingly since engaging in investigations of hauntings – that there is some inexplicable energy which can operate within a terrestrial framework, yet independently of chronological time. Since nothing is known about this force or its laws, it seems extremely foolish to begin or continue tampering with it at the present stage of ignorance. The kind of casual 'spirit-raising' or 'table-turning' which are indulged in as a light-hearted party game are as sensible as throwing stones at a live bomb or grabbing a bare electric wire with a wet hand.

What needs to be done. I think, is a systematic and thorough investigation of psychic phenomena, with some ordered attempt to catalogue the data† – i.e. the different types of manifestation, classification of activities in relation to particular groups, degree and timing of manifestations, plus any historical information available as background. Much more research needs to be undertaken and correlation of findings before the stage is reached when so-called 'contacts' are attempted. This is a personal opinion only. I am well aware that it may not be shared.

The bingo hall still has its ghost, I believe, though I have no recent information on the subject of its behaviour.

Tony Freeman, the young journalist mentioned earlier in this chapter, gave me a small ghost story of his own.

In his early childhood his family moved to a new house on a council estate east of Northampton. Before the housing development took place, the land had been part of an old country park; however, by 1950 the town had encroached far enough for the new estate to be on the municipal boundary. The original park had contained a royal deer park and hunting area, though all that remained when the Freemans first moved in was the old Manor House, a few farm buildings, the remains of the wooded deer park and a large

† Since writing the above, much sound research and classification has been undertaken by existing psychical field workers, in particular, the members of the Society for Psychical Research of Great Britain.

lake with a derelict boathouse at one end.

One afternoon in summer, the child Tony (aged six or seven at the time) with several friends was at play in the park. The weather was warm, the air drowsy and the boy stopped on the bank of the lake to gaze into the water, hoping to see a few tadpoles. He thought his friends were behind him, sitting or standing on the grass and was therefore not particularly surprised when he felt a hand touch him on the back between the shoulder blades and then a firm push which sent him headlong into the water. It was hardly deep enough to drown him, but the lad was young and afraid. He came up, yelled in fear and anger at his friends, then managed to scramble out. It was not until he had done so that he realised the other children were nowhere near: when he had stopped to gaze, they had continued walking and were now about fifty yards ahead along the lakeshore. It took them a few moments to run back to the dripping Anthony and in retrospect the latter says that the culprit would not have had time to duck him and rejoin the group before he saw where they were. There was no other person within running distance; his friends saw no one else although they could see him. All the children strongly denied responsibility for the incident. Tony Freeman concluded his story by saying, 'There might have been a puff of wind which blew my shirt against my back, although I have never before or since felt a puff of wind which had fingers.'

Ghosts, though, have been known to push, as Mr Pedder of Finchingfield can attest.

If you think the last a disconcerting experience, consider that of the Haywood family of Oundle.

The Haywoods own a hardware shop in the middle of the town and reside in the house attached to it. The whole property occupies part of the site of an old monastery, and it is thought to be this portion of the area's history from which the haunting springs.

Mr Tony Haywood showed me around the house and in particular one bedroom which appears to be more affected than the rest. One night when his mother-in-law was sleeping in the room she felt something breathing down her neck. Somewhat sharply she ordered the breather to 'Go away!' and thereafter slept undisturbed. Another time the Haywoods themselves were using the room. Both awoke in the night hearing the sound of an opening door followed by footsteps, and thought their young son had left his room to go to the lavatory. On checking, however, they found the child sound asleep in his bed. Again when their daughter got up one night, she experienced a similar incident. A particularly nasty event occurred when Mrs Haywood was sleeping alone, in the haunted bedroom; she heard footsteps approaching the bed and then *walking right through it* and out the other side. All the manifestations in this room were at one side of it, and would seem to be connected with a regular route or passageway which once existed there and across which the bed now stands.

Another interesting feature of this haunting is that during the last war the place was occupied by a Catholic family and on one occasion a church meeting was being held in the sitting-room (now a bedroom). At one point the meeting was disturbed and almost disrupted by the sounds of fighting arising from the downstairs premises. Investigation proved that nothing unusual was taking place in the lower regions and the sounds were attributed to the period of the monasteries' dissolution, when fighting frequently took place between the King's men and dispossessed monks.

It is now twelve months since anything out of the ordinary occurred on these premises, so in all probability the ghostly record has played itself out.

This is not the case in a house in Warmington. The Manor House is beautiful, dignified and of great age and must be a delightful house to own and live in, as its owner confirmed. A grey lady has been seen upstairs, however, and footsteps have been heard, doors heard to open and all the usual paraphernalia of an ordinary house-haunting are present. The one unusual feature of this one is that the ghostly lady favours the stairs; and the stairs are said to have come from Fotheringhay Castle. I thought the staircase looked later in period than sixteenth century, so the waiting lady was perhaps not a lady-in-waiting, nor yet the Lady herself.

A similar Fotheringhay echo appears in two other establishments in the locality, and certainly in one case I believe the tradition is more wishful than truthful. But the Manor House at Warmington is very attractive, with a happy, relaxed atmosphere; whatever ghost inhabits it has not disturbed its tranquillity.

A weird little tale came from the manager of Barclay's Bank in Oundle. Mr and Mrs Ogden at one time lived in a house known as The Lodge, situated between Fotheringhay and Nassington. During a period of illness Mrs Ogden was confined to bed for a time, but prior to this certain minor manifestations had taken place; knocks had been heard several times on windows which looked out on to neighbouring property. These, though irritating, were not particularly alarming. Mrs Ogden's experience fell into a different category.

A pair of candlesticks stood on the dressing-table in her bedroom, and while she looked at them, one of the candles moved out of the candlestick and fell to the floor. If your mind is now boggling at this thought, be comforted: mine did also. *How* did it move? The candlestick fell over, perhaps? Apparently not. The candle lifted out of the stick and then fell.

Mrs Ogden called out for her husband and he, understandably, thought she must have been mistaken. Candles do not levitate; it is not in the nature of candles. He replaced the offending object and withdrew.

Some time afterwards the Ogdens' young son came in to be with his mother, and it was while he was in the room that the occurrence was repeated – the candle lifted out of the candlestick and fell. This time the child also saw the activity.

Later the same morning while Mrs Ogden was still in bed she felt the bottom of the bed sink, as though someone had sat upon it. She thought the dog had jumped on to the bedfoot, but nothing was there.

The house has only one story which could account for the haunting – that of a fifteen-year-old boy who had hanged himself from the top of the stairs.

'I do not,' Mr Ogden said, 'believe in ghosts.' But he had more of twinkle than of truth in his eye as he spoke.

I was still ruminating on this strange tale when I visited Colonel and Mrs McMichael of Glapthorne. Their own house is an old and pleasant structure, converted from the former village smithy, with the intrinsic character of the place skilfully retained. Before they occupied their present home, they lived near the river Nene in Oundle, in a house appropriately called Nene Cottage.

It was not, I believe, a house which Mrs McMichael had particularly liked when the couple moved in, but it was thought to be convenient at the time. One room in the house Mrs McMichael felt particular distaste for – a spare bedroom – though in the event it turned out to be a front room (used by the McMichaels as a drawing-room) which turned out to be different from the others. This room looked out on to the roadway.

The McMichaels are sensitive and cultured people, with the warmth and charm one associates with the Scots. They are not, I should say, given to exaggerated or unduly romanticised reactions. Their story of the ghosts of Nene Cottage is therefore particularly striking.

It appears that from time to time the handle of the drawing-room door would rattle, this event frequently occurring at tea time, and the rattling suggested to Mrs McMichael the presence of children. The knob was turned in the manner used by a small child when it cannot quite reach its objective. Anyone who has lived with small children recognises this sound. The presences were also 'sensed' or 'felt' in the house; the family cat also showing signs of this sensitivity.

I have mentioned earlier this sense of presence; an indefinable thing which I suspect is connected with the occupation of space or displacement of air – akin perhaps to the innate knowledge of *size* which each of us possesses. Every normally intelligent human is aware of his own body size, of where and how his physical structure terminates – hence the common sensation following amputation, that the missing limb is still present in its former shape and size.

Not only do we possess this awareness of our own physical size, we are also aware of the body-space of others – of their displacement of air and (perhaps) the consequent alteration in surface pressure upon our own bodies in the presence of theirs. Hence the awareness of another presence in a room which we occupy, even though there may be no physical, visible evidence of that presence: *something* is there which is not ourselves or the furniture, or the fire or the cat or the dog.

I believe it was so in Nene Cottage. Occasionally, when the McMichaels were having tea in the drawing-room, the door handle would rattle as though someone were struggling with it, and Mrs McMichael (who by this time had grown attached to her ghosts) would call to them to come in. There were, she thought, two of them.

When the McMichaels left, Nene Cottage was empty for two years and the incidents of life there were beginning to fade into memory. It was therefore with surprise that Mrs McMichael answered the telephone one day to find the new owner of her former home, a complete stranger, on the line. 'Have you ever,' asked the latter, 'seen a ghost here? I have seen two small children in the passage . . .'

One wonders who they were, these young children, that their pattern of life should have remained in the house. Later publicity, I gather, was loud, raucous and distasteful and one wonders if the delicacy of this particular imprint has been destroyed.

Mrs Mary McMichael is a descendant of Rob Roy, an interesting character to have in one's ancestry. She also appears to have a 'sixth sense' – that Celtic quality which can cause its possessor an uncomfortable prescience, giving him an ability occasionally to sidestep conscious time. It's a precocious thing, coming and going unpredictably and being a bit like love in that it 'longest stays where sorest chidden; laughs and flies when pressed and bidden'.

On one occasion Mrs McMichael was engaged in some cleaning activities in the local church prior, I think, to a festival. I imagine several ladies must have volunteered to help out in this way, for this is part of the unseen work which goes on behind the scenes of parish celebrations. Mary McMichael was alone in the church, and had been working around a pew on hands and knees and was therefore well out of sight of anyone entering from the west or far end of the nave.

The vicar of the parish was a serious, well-liked man, with a sense of fun, and Mrs McMichael assumed it was he whose footsteps she heard approaching down the length of the nave. A mischievous thought occurred to her to hurl her scrubbing brush in front of the incumbent just as he passed the pew. A scrubbing brush hurtling out from an empty pew would have surprised him considerably.

While she was considering the question to hurl or not to hurl, the footsteps drew level with the pew, passed by and continued towards the chancel. It was Mary McMichael who had the shock. There was absolutely no human being in sight. Unable to believe her ears, she walked to the vestry to investigate, but that proved to be as empty as the rest of the building. No solution has ever been suggested to explain this manifestation, though the strong monastic tradition in the area may have had something to do with it.

You cannot go anywhere in the Oundle area without encountering echoes of either the monasteries or of Mary Stuart, Queen of Scotland. Fotheringhay was a power in its high days; when it was brought low it became a pile of rubbish, a treasure-trove to be pillaged by local peasantry and gentry alike. Whoever had edifices in the process of building looked to the ruined castle to supply his needs.

There had been no need to demolish Fotheringhay Castle; it had served a useful purpose as a State prison and an occasional home for passing royal monarchs on progress, but it was the former fact which condemned it in the eyes of James I. As Nottingham had been the Castle of Care for Richard III, so had Fotheringhay for James's mother. Mary had spent her last months here, and the castle's great hall was the last thing she saw on earth. The very thought of the place, the mere sound of its name must have made the son sick. He ordered its destruction and the castle was dismantled and finally reduced to a pile of rubble, over which the turf spread, at first thinly and then in depth. Now all that shows of that distant power is a grassy mound surrounded by thistle and flowering thorns. Legend states that Mary herself planted the first thistles there to remind her of Scotland. Legend has been kinder to her than to that other monarch of Fotheringhay, Richard Plantagenet.

The castle timber and stones became spread around the neighbourhood, and some of it went to rebuild an old inn in Oundle, the Tabret. Panelling was built into the bedrooms and stones into the walls. By tradition part of the great staircase also went into the building – the staircase Mary descended on 8 February 1587. I have seen that staircase in the rebuilt inn – now known as the Talbot – and doubt its dating. It would seem nearly a hundred years later in period than the story suggests, though this is opinion and there are other views on the subject. It bears on one of the balusters at its head the tiny imprint of a crown, said to have been made by the pressure of the royal ring. One suspects this is tourists' stuff, but it adds a nice touch of drama to the stairway.

What is factual is the Talbot's date. The place was established in 638 as a hospitium associated with the monastery and here the monks supplied travellers with food, drink and shelter. It was rebuilt in 1626.

It is an intriguing building which carries its age lightly, though one cannot say it has become fossilised in any particular period. Modification and amendment have been carried out at intevals, as required. Unfortunately, whenever alterations are made the ghost of a woman appears. She haunts two of the bedrooms and the upper part of the staircase and has been seen on many occasions, although always. I understand, by men. Her appearance does not vary. She is described as wearing a white dress with a grey shawl and a white cap, and she stands at the foot of the bed, looking at its occupant. Usually the phenomenon occurs some time between February and April.

After a fire escape was added in the hotel, the spectre appeared to three different men who stayed in the haunted rooms in succession. On another occasion a man came down from one of these rooms and said he had had a terrible night and been quite unable to sleep because of a woman sobbing in the next bedroom. No woman was staying on that floor of the hotel that night. Many visitors have heard the sound of weeping, however.

Locally it is thought that the ghost is either that of the Queen or of one of her ladies and the haunt-pattern is a replay of the night before the execution.

The affected staircase is in two flights, an upper and a lower. When I first set eyes on it, I felt markedly that the upper part was that affected, and Mr Stewart, manager of the Talbot confirmed this. I felt also that the woman who had been seen in the bedrooms (one of these rooms had a more pronounced 'atmosphere' than the other) was a shorter woman than Mary and older – and indeed may not even have been of the same period. I did not see or hear anything at all while in the hotel and the word 'felt' in this context is intended as an expression of an intuitive reaction.

I spoke to an employee who has worked for many years in the hotel. Mrs Ives has slept in one of the haunted rooms and she had an experience as alarming although different from that of the inn's male guests. She thought that someone was holding her down on the bed. It was, she told me, as though a hand were pressing her back on to the bed and she was unable either to move or call out. She was quite unable to switch on the light. This incident occurred in about 1965.

The most recent sighting of the ghost (by a man) was in 1972, although after recent renovations to the Talbot it is possible that the manifestation will be encountered again.

There is a large picture on the wall of the hotel lounge, depicting Mary of Scotland on the night before the execu-

*The Talbot Hotel, Oundle*

133

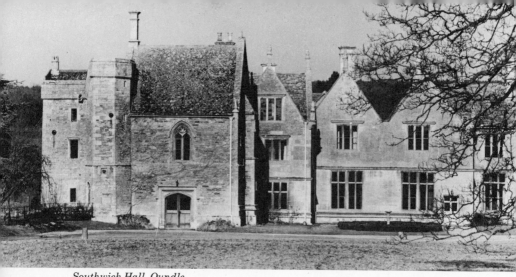

*Southwick Hall, Oundle*

tion. It has some drama, this portrait, for the Queen is seated, chin on hand, gazing out of the picture, with an expression of weary sadness. It is also a fairly accurate portrait of the woman as her contemporaries recorded her, though it is not, of course, a contemporary picture.

The week before I visited the hotel, the manager with a group of guests had been in the lounge discussing the fact the ghost had not been seen for several months. One of the group at the bar had laughed and said, 'Where is Mary?' For a moment there was silence, then the picture on the wall fell with a resounding crash to the floor. Coincidence? There was a strong reaction from the group at the bar and the badinage abruptly ceased.

I found echoes of the Scottish queen again three miles from Fotheringhay at the village of Southwick.

Southwick Hall is a small but exquisite country mansion with a long history. The house was founded some time between 1300 and 1310, and some rebuilding was undertaken in the years 1571–80. Later still, in the eighteenth century, extensive redecoration was carried out. The result is a harmonious blending of medieval, Tudor and eighteenth-century work.

It is a house of surprises and there are some singularly attractive features both of structure and furnishing. I was delighted to find a portrait of Edward IV which was new to me. This was a print of an original which had once hung here before being translated to the National Portrait Gallery. Two rooms carry fine Adam fireplaces; another, known as the Oak Room, retains its original Elizabethan panelling. It was in this room that I saw samples of nineteenth-century clothing laid out – items which had belonged to ancestors of the Capron family.

The medieval house contained a chapel and crypt. Since the Reformation the former has been known as the Gothic Room, one of the entrances to which is by a stone spiral staircase. The whole of this square tower block was added to the original house between 1320 and 1358.

Southwick Hall has been owned by members of the same family since it was built, though the inheritance has not always been by direct descent. The Capron family, who are the present owners, have descent from the Lynnes and Knyvets of Southwick who built the hall, and the Capron name was originally 'de Caperun' – one who came over with the Conqueror.

When the connection between an occupying family and an old house has been so long and continuous, the history of one is the history of the other; the house reflects and echoes the changing fortunes of that family. It was so with Sawston Hall in Cambridgeshire; it is equally true of Southwick Hall.

The family at Southwick were Catholic in Elizabethan times, and since Fotheringhay was only three miles away across country (even today the lantern tower of that village's church may be seen from the hall) it was natural that the Catholic prisoner in the castle should be a focus of interest and sympathy.

There is a local tradition that Fotheringhay Castle and Southwick Hall were once connected by an underground passageway and that a certain amount of traffic took place between the two places. Since Mary may well have found difficulty in celebrating Mass under the eyes of her jailers at Fotheringhay, it is likely that once or twice she succeeded in reaching Southwick to attend Mass in the little chapel there. One can imagine the risk and the secrecy with which such visits would be surrounded. To stand in the stone chapel, with its altar space occupied now by a marble table, its panelled walls hung with miniatures, is to feel an overwhelming closeness to the past. One waits for the door behind to open and for the swift rush of steps towards the altar. There is still, in that place, a slight but indefinable tension, as of waiting, or of danger.

I spoke my thoughts aloud. '*She* must have been here at some time.'

It was Miss Elaine Capron who satisfied my curiosity.

On one occasion when Miss Capron was in the chapel, she thought she heard footsteps approaching the room. It occurred to her that some unauthorised person had come into the house and was now prowling around uninvited. She therefore concealed herself behind a curtain and waited to see who was the prowler. What, or rather *whom*, she thought she saw caused her to rise to her feet. A tallish woman entered, slim in build, straight-backed, wearing a long dark dress with the collar upright and pointed at the back. She wore no headdress. The woman appeared to walk to the altar and stand before it, hands clasped together in front of her. She stood so for a few seconds, then moved through the Priest's Room to the stone spiral staircase and began to descend. Elaine Capron, after a paralysed minute, hastened after her. But the turret stair was empty. No one was in that part of the building save Miss Capron herself.

Make of this what you will. Mary the Queen? Who can say? The physical description fits.

Southwick has other echoes which may spring from the same era in its history or may be of a different period. One such is in the Oak Room where I had seen the parasols and embroidered waistcoats of the early nineteenth century. One member of the family who had slept in this room thought he saw a child there, who walked through the wall facing his bed. This wall probably held a door at an earlier date. Before being told that this was one of the haunted rooms, I suspected as much and remarked upon it to my guide. No real way of knowing, still less of explaining how this instinct works. Perhaps 'tension' is the best word to describe the difference in feeling between a haunted and an unhaunted area. The degree of tension varies from the slight to the considerable and sometimes it seems to be passive, sometimes active. The state appears to reflect the degree of haunting which is taking place there.

There was one other room which had produced manifestations. There seemed nothing remarkable about it, save again for a degree of tautness in the feeling of the place. I was told that persons sleeping there had been disturbed by a door persistently opening. When it was closed it would re-open. A faulty catch, you might think, and so it could have been, but when a heavy table was placed against this door, the table was later found pushed away and the door open. There was when I saw it another heavy piece of furniture against the door, and the latter was firmly shut.

Southwick Hall has known history certainly. A member of the family, George Lynne, attended Mary's funeral and returned home to Southwick afterwards. Elizabeth's spies apparently did not suspect him of involvement in any of the many Catholic plots to overthrow her.

Arising from this incident is perhaps the most intriguing part of Southwick's story. It is said that after the interment of the Queen, her burial certificate was given into the care of George Lynne, and taken back by him to Southwick Hall. The certificate has never come to light, and is presumed to be still concealed somewhere in the old house. The legend is firmly established, and one must conclude that is is built on a factual foundation; somewhere in the building may be a document of priceless historical value. Such a thought invests every stone and panel of the house with unique interest.

Southwick is a fascinating house. However romantic its past, it is invested now by a mellow grace, a warm kindness, which seems to spring from the members of the family currently living there. Unconsciously perhaps they interpret and express Southwick because they are the current part of its long story.

A few miles to the south-east stand the ruins of Barnwell Castle, which like Southwick Hall is a product of medieval building.

The castle was completed in 1264 by Reginald le Moine, and though small as Norman castles go, is still a massive structure, its ruined walls and bastioned gatehouse forming an impressive background for the Elizabethan manor house which faces it across the eighty-five yards of dividing garden.

Difficult to appraise one structure without the other. The two, medieval and Tudor, balance each other in rare complement and each with a mellow beauty which, during my visit there, the evening light of late June enhanced.

The ghost story, if that is the correct term for the strange experience of Mr Tom Litchfield, concerns the castle. Mr Litchfield is a Northamptonshire historian of some note and a local farmer on the Barnwell estate. His antiquarian interest in the castle was, I suspect, deepened by local stories or questionings, over the years.

On at least two occasions in recent years, local residents (one of them a police constable on patrol in the castle area at the time; the other the village postmaster walking his dog near the ruins late at night) have reported a sound 'like a rushing wind' which whirled by them out of an apparently still night, leaving an equal stillness in its wake.

In the case of the postmaster, his dog had broken away from him and run up to the castle and he had followed to bring the animal back. He was approaching the ruin's southern side when the manifestation occurred. In the postmaster's own words, 'Suddenly I was conscious of a noise and sensation like a wind rushing by. At the same time my dog raced by me towards the road, her hair standing up. She was waiting and trembling on the doorstep of the post office when I got home.'

One further reference had been made to the castle's atmosphere, and this also by a former policeman who had patrolled the area. Some time around 1934, ex-Police Constable W. Kendall had said (the fact was recalled and recounted to me by Tom Litchfield), 'There is one place in the old castle where I wouldn't go for all the tea in China.' The area referred to was apparently the north-east tower.

Some time in 1948, Tom Litchfield and a friend of his (the man was an engineer, with no historical appreciation but some psychic ability) had determined to probe the stories of the castle. They therefore decided to experiment with Ouija, and conducted at least three séances, two in the Litchfields' home, the third in the castle itself. For the latter experiment they chose the north-east tower.

Following each séance, Mr Litchfield made detailed notes on its conduct and results and I have seen this textual record.

The first séance took place at the Litchfield house in Barnwell village on 20 September 1948. Almost at once some contact was made, and from replies to questions it appeared that the first respondent was an Abbot of Ramsey Abbey. He gave brief answers to questions, from which it was apparent that the castle had been used as a court of justice and summary execution in the fourteenth century. (Tom Litchfield afterwards verified this fact in the *Chartularies of the Abbey of Ramsey*, ed. by W. H. Hart and Lyon – Historical MSS Commission.)

At the point when execution was mentioned during this first séance, a change of respondent appeared to take place. Replies to subsequent questions became longer, elaborated and couched in recognisably archaic terms. I will quote here from Tom Litchfield's textual record of the proceedings.

Q. Who is speaking now?
A. Marie, *uxor*† Le Moine.
Q. What did you mean by horror and untimely death? [An earlier answer had used this phrase in relation to the castle's history.]
A. In the dungeon, in the chest there.
Q. What is there in the chest?
A. The remnants of a ruined life.
Q. Whose?
A. Mine. Marie *uxor* Le Moine.
Q. What year?
A. *Anno* 1245.
Q. Was there a castle then?
A. In process. [Barnwell castle was completed in 1265. It was probably in building in 1245.]
Q. How was your life ruined?
A. Heathen rule enforcing a brutish captivity.
Q. Who imprisoned you?
A. Secret. I can never betray my soul's secret.
Q. Can you tell us anything else?
A. Pray very hard. Terrible death it was; he came quietly. Play not for time; he will win the race.

This marked the end of the first séance. According to Tom Litchfield's subsequent researches, the wife of one of the Le Moine lords was certainly named Marie.

† *Uxor*, i.e. wife.

There is also a local legend – without, as far as Mr Litchfield can ascertain, any factually verifiable basis – that Berengarius Le Moine, son of the castle's builder, walled up a woman alive into Barnwell castle. It is also factually correct that Marie Le Moine died in 1245, according to the local records.

A further séance was held in the same house on 30 September 1948, and the following is a transcript of proceedings.

Q. Who are you?
A. I am the left bastion. I am Reginald Le Moine.
Q. What is there in the left bastion?
A. My successor will inform you.
Q. Who is your successor?
A. The second bastion named Berengarius Le Moine.
Q. What is there in the left bastion? [At this point there appears to have been a change of respondent. The next speaker was apparently Berengarius Le Moine.]
A. The horrid remains of suppression which befell an honest lord. William forced my reason.
Q. Who is William?
A. We call him covert in Ramsey. [N.B. Berengarius Le Moine was compelled to cede the castle and lands back to the Abbey of Ramsey in the person of Abbot William of Godmanchester in 1276. 'Covert' in this context appears to mean secretive. Abbot William was reputed to be careful with money.]

Other exchanges in this séance appear to relate to a later period of time. They are interesting but irrelevant to this particular enquiry.

A third (and last) séance was held in the north-east tower of the castle itself, and took place about 9.00 p.m. on the night of 9 November 1948.

In one place in this tower a broken piece of masonry forms a flat area; this the men found suitable for their purpose; the Ouija symbols were arranged accordingly and a storm lantern placed beside the improvised table. The session was short but terrifying.

*Barnwell Castle*

Q. I wish to ask further questions. Are you willing?
A. Yes. The soul ascends to realms immortal but the flesh to worms most vile.
Q. Who is speaking?
A. I am the second bastion, Berengarius Le Moine.
Q. What have you to say?
A. I will fire to warn you.

Almost immediately there followed above the investigators' heads in the ruined tower a sharp crack like a pistol or the crack of a whip. The friends saw then, or thought they saw, the head and upper torso of a monk in the inner doorway to the courtyard. Both men hurriedly left the tower.

Tom Litchfield's friend lived seven miles away from Barnwell. He returned home, but in the early hours of the morning when in his bedroom, he heard the same report, as of a whiplash, which both men had heard earlier.

There was at least one sequel to this remarkable story. Later investigation took Mr Litchfield to All Saints Church at Sawtrey, some ten miles from Barnwell. Here the Le Moine family is commemorated in a brass tablet. Above it is an insignia in the shape of the upper torso of a monk carrying in his hand a whip.

This is one of the most extraordinary stories I have encountered, and particularly interesting because of the factual and verifiable detail. The quality of the language in which the replies were given seems significant. Neither of the investigators would have been likely to use archaisms of this kind.

There are other points of interest. Consider the answers to some of the investigators' questions. In response to the demand for identification one reply was:

'I am the left hand bastion. I am Reginald Le Moine.'

The bastion referred to can only be one of those at the gatehouse. The formation of this gatehouse is unusual in that it possesses three bastions instead of two. There is a bastion to left and right of the gate itself, but farther left still stands a third. This bastion is something of a mystery, for it has a slit window aperture on the outside which cannot be seen from within, and there appear to be ten to twelve feet of space unaccounted for in the thickness of the outer wall. Of a dungeon in any other part of the ruined castle, there is no sign.

During one of the séances, answers purporting to come from Marie Le Moine indicate that she was murdered by being walled up in the castle, which was then 'in process' of building. The location of death is given as a chest in the dungeon. This respondent refused to say by whom she was imprisoned, referring in this context to its being her 'soul's secret'.

Berengarius Le Moine, in his turn, replied to a question about the contents of the left bastion by suggesting that whatever was concealed there was a result of some madness on his part resulting from pressure by Abbot William of Godmanchester or Ramsey. Could that madness have included killing his wife – if Marie Le Moine was his wife? No reason was given at any time by any of the respondents during the séances for a murder of this kind.

There are one or two inexplicable factors: Marie Le Moine's references to a secret; the absence of any dungeon in the castle, though at this period of Norman building a dungeon was as much a necessity as a gatehouse; the repeated puzzling references to the left hand bastion; and the thickness of the wall of the far left bastion of the gatehouse.

One further oddity. The 'rushing wind' noted by two or three witnesses seems usually to have been encountered near the gatehouse.

Since the total story is so extraordinary, my guesses are unlikely to increase the wildness of the tale by more than a fraction. I would suggest:

1. That for a reason unknown, Berengarius Le Moine may have had Marie Le Moine walled up in the castle (a little late in time for this kind of barbarism, but not unheard of).
2. That the thickness of the wall in the far left tower is large enough to conceal a room.
3. That a dungeon must have existed somewhere in the castle, and the only likely place is this same left hand tower.
4. That the fact that the manifestations (those stirred up by Tom Litchfield and his friend appear to be exceptions) mainly seem to have been near the gatehouse and its towers, points to the original story of the haunting being sited in this area.

On a last inspection of the castle ruins in the warm half-light of the June evening, only one area really troubled me and produced the familiar feeling of tension and unease. The north-east tower, where the séance was held and the monk appeared? Not at all. I thought it gloomy, forbidding, but nothing more. The area which actually felt 'wrong', where there seemed to be a sense of discomfort, was that around the far left tower (note: not the *left* bastion, but the *far left* bastion, that with the unusually thick wall). At this time, I had not seen the texts of the séances and was not therefore using hindsight.

I would suggest that if ever this tower is excavated, a hidden room between the walls is a strong possibility. An even stronger one is that it will contain the skeleton of a woman.

Tom Litchfield had one further story to tell me, which was a gentle thing after the Gothic horror of the last.

It concerns Woodford Church and two local grammar-school boys who were photographing inside the church. One assumes these activities were part of some school project or other. In the course of their visit, they took a photograph of the altar. When the picture was developed, the lads were much surprised to see the kneeling figure of a man before the altar, and that the figure was recognisably wearing boots. No one had been kneeling in front of the altar when the photograph was taken, of that they were certain. The predecessor of the rector holding the living at the time had been used to wearing boots, however, and it had been his daily habit to go into the church to pray.

It is extraordinary that the camera lens can record such phenomena when the human eye does not.

Once or twice during the course of our several conversations, Mr Litchfield had alluded to a local family by the name of Montague. Eventually we visited the small church where their memorial stood and where members of the family were buried. They proved to be the Earls of Sandwich, descended from that same Edward Montague, Earl of Sandwich, who died in the battle of Sole Bay and who has persistently dogged the pages of this book.

'He was,' said Tom Litchfield, 'found floating face upwards in the water some time after the battle. He was unrecognisable and was only identified by the Garter insignia which he wore.' A sad end for a bonny gentleman: and for the little red-haired maid of Southwold.

I left Northamptonshire with great reluctance, and it is impossible to describe the blend of impressions which commended it so strongly to me; warmth? friendliness? history? More than these, I think. Tradition, perhaps, and a kind of rural pride which has long, long roots. It is a beautiful county also, but about this I propose to say nothing.

# Conclusion

After a year's work on the ghosts of the East Anglian region – a year of talking, writing, reading, asking questions, listening to answers and just plain standing still and trying to apprehend with all one's senses, the inapprehendible – what conclusions have been reached?

For a time nothing fell into place. One sought for theories, and having found them, tested them out against evidence, only to have the whole structure collapse on the next investigation when a completely different type of phenomenon was involved. After a while it seemed that before seeking theories of how psychic phenomena work, one must first classify the phenomena themselves.

There are, I believe, several different types of supernatural event and these fall roughly into one or other of the following categories.

1.  Pattern-hauntings (where constant repetition of a routine in life has established a fixed pattern).
2.  Single event (where one dramatic event has occurred – murder, suicide, etc. – producing an intense emotion).
3.  'One-off' manifestation (where the manifestation occurs once only and never again – e.g. a warning or farewell).
4.  Primitive, archaic or racial-memory manifestation (the phenomenon occurring in many different areas of the country and having a symbolic or magical meaning, e.g. Black Shuck).
5.  Poltergeist (noisy demonstration involving use of considerable energy).
6.  Elemental (as primitive as No. 5, but without violence, often characterised by a feeling of evil or hostility).
7.  Historical (sometimes of the 'pattern' type, also, but frequently registering a historic incident or personality).
8.  'Miracle' or God-given sign (resulting in an appearance of divine intervention: see the Scampton guide).
9.  Large scale replay (common ground with Nos. 7 and 1, but this is on a wholesale scale: see battle of Naseby).
10. Death-survival (where the recently dead appear to return to their life environment, sometimes by way of farewell, sometimes as an announcement of their death or as an attempt to reach the living. This is frequently overlapped by No. 3).

Almost all the instances of so-called haunting recorded in this book fall into one or more of the categories given above.

Within the categories the mechanics – if one may use the term in this context – seem to run to a formula. Pattern-hauntings, for instance, usually involve practical and simple manifestations, like the opening of doors, the sound of footsteps, manipulation of lights, etc. Occasionally there is the movement of objects (the candle movements near Nassington, the sale goods in the Royston Oxfam shop) or unusual sounds (the woman sobbing in the Talbot Inn, Oundle; the sound of metal falling at Eynesbury), but I suspect that in the first two cases the movements were attempts to attract attention; in the second two, they were endless repeats of a single incident – which point to a distinct overlapping of categories. To suggest that a haunting may be an attempt to attract attention raises another set of questions, to which I will turn presently.

There are apparently a number of forms which manifestation can take, and the following are examples which come to mind:

1.  Materialisation – the actual appearance of a representation of the form occupied during life.
2.  Audible – including speech, laughter, weeping, music or the general noise of human activity.
3.  Locomotive – the movement of objects and/or persons.
4.  Smells – varying from flower and incense to that of food, burning or decay.
5.  Physical touch or sensation – the feeling of cobwebs or a hand pushing or pressing.
6.  Mist – usually referred to as 'grey', 'damp', 'clinging'.
7.  Temperature drop – a frequent, almost invariable accompaniment.
8.  A sensation of 'presence', of being not alone, or of being watched.

Again, manifestations can be a combination of several of these components.

To accept the possibility of a haunting being an attempt to attract the attention of the living, presupposes that one believes in personal survival of death. When I began this book this was a subject on which I had reached no decision. Certain events in my own personal and family experience had led me to think that death of the physical body might not mean an end of individual awareness – that a part of the psyche might remain in existence in some area which was not the terrestrial, three-dimensional, chronological concept in which man lives from cradle to grave.

Now that I have completed this work with its attendant researches, I feel fairly certain that there is some survival of physical death by the individual awareness – though whether for a prolonged period I am not sure. Certainly for a while after the body's death, it seems possible for the psyche to function as it had in life, and for it to return to the scenes of its human participation. There are many instances of this in these pages – the old man at Kessingland, the American airman, are two examples.

In certain cases, the contact with the old, remembered place is prolonged, as though the surviving awareness were unable to escape from a deep bond formed in life – a constricting life-habit – the servant girl at Southwold, the grocer at Royston, the miser at Thaxted. All these infect their surroundings with the sense of something *aware and existent*, though without physical reality; and in most such cases there appear to be attempts to attract the attention of the living.

These seem subtly different from hauntings which appear superficially similar – the 'pattern' haunts, the ghostly monks and nuns, the sets of sounds and movements which rehearse or replay specific incidents. The 'existent' group is less predictable in its activities; one cannot tell what will happen next and there seems no set pattern, other than one occasionally imposed by an anniversary.

I think, therefore, that certain ghostly manifestations are the result of recordings by material surroundings; I believe others are indications of survival of death by an intelligent awareness. And since one can hardly select a few only to survive, to accept this theory implies an acceptance of the general survival of physical death by human personality.

Whether or not one accepts this premise, one is still left with a vast number of recorded and apparently authentic hauntings which appear inexplicable by the light of contemporary knowledge of natural laws. According to the present state of such knowledge, one must say that ghosts do not exist, that hauntings do not take place, because it is impossible to offer any scientific explanation for such activities. It is hardly necessary to point out that in Copernicus's time it was impossible to offer any scientific explanation for the encircling of the sun by the earth – not because such a fact was untrue but because of the limited and incomplete nature of human knowledge at that time. Similarly in the year 1900, a suggestion of the possibility of television or space flight would have been considered fantasy. It is the development of knowedge which releases truth from its prison. (Michelangelo said that every block of marble had a statue waiting within for its release.)

There remains the mystery of how psychic manifestations occur. In the light of the evidence collected, it seems apparent that nothing can occur without the use of energy. All the customary ghostly activities require expenditure of energy – speech, movement, materialisation – and since a non-physical entity is not possessed of physical energy, the activities must be powered by other means. One such energy form is heat, another is electricity. In almost every manifestation we have seen that heat-loss is present at the time; and in several cases of haunting, the normal electricity supply has been affected (the Black Lion at Northampton) or electrical equipment has been disturbed (the motor-cars carrying the haunted chair of Mrs Hutt). It looks then as though psychic activities not only need and use power in the form of energy before they can take place, but that it is possible for existing forms of power (energy) to be adapted or transmuted for that purpose. And I cannot begin to guess how that process operates. Is it arbitrarily triggered off in the case of re-broadcast hauntings? Or consciously used in the case of actual presence hauntings? And what of the historical manifestations, the haunting of Cromwell's cavalry, Nell Gwynne, Mary Queen of Scots? The questions fall like rain at the end of summer.

There is also the influence of Time – that strange pattern maker, whose properties, in spite of Einstein, are only barely or fractionally understood.

Perhaps Time instead of being a straight line as we regard it, a route leading directly from A to Z, the shortest distance between baby's rattle and the tombstone, perhaps Time is a grid laid across the cubic pattern of Space and either cubic in its own form, or able to move its grid pattern across and through the other. There would then be freedom to travel both in space and time once the physical limitation of flesh were discarded. Fantasy? So was moon-flight once.

One comes at last to the ultimate point – that not I or you or any living being knows what a ghost is or what is meant by haunting.

*Something* there is, though, and the screen of time is barely enough to hide our one world from that other.

# Index